"The lowdown on the odds and the odd-balls in Las Vegas."

CNN Television

"Belongs at the top of the reading list for everyone on both sides of the tables... told with wit and charm."

Las Vegas Source

"Where most sequels lag, this sequel is in front of the pack!"

American Radio Network

"Tells more than all the others we've seen about the up-and-down casino industry."

Loose Change Magazine

"A storehouse of facts and funny–tragic experiences that makes this book an informative and very readable experience."

Las Vegas Sun

"Well researched... it's amazing all these things really happen out there."

WBAL, Baltimore

"Almost as fun as being there."

WLS, Chicago

"Loved both books... can't wait for your next one."

WKRC, Cincinnati

LAS VEGAS
BEHIND THE TABLES!
PART 2

BARNEY VINSON

GOLLEHON
GRAND RAPIDS, MICHIGAN

Library of Congress Catalog Card Number: 86-80659

ISBN 0-914839-25-X
(International Standard Book Number)

Photo of author, courtesy of Gemini Studios

Contents

Acknowledgements

This sequel of "Las Vegas Behind The Tables" could not have been written without the help of many people: Jeff Burbank, Tony Cook, Howard Cornbleth, Jim Darrough, Paul Endy, Dennis Gomes, Phil Hevener, Michael Hoover, Donn Knepp, Jay Love, John Martie, Russ McLennan, Dan Mead, Johnny Moss, Dick Odessky, Neil Ohriner, Puggy Pearson, Lee Pete, Sonny Reizner, Russell Scott, Harold Tuttle, Vic Vickrey, Valerie Wagmeister, Daniel Wade, and Steve Wynn.

I would like to thank my publisher, John Gollehon, whose dream it was to bring this book to life. To Sergio Lalli, my special thanks for "service above and beyond the call of greenbacks." To Dennis Amerine and Mike Rumbolz of the Nevada Gaming Control Board, my appreciation for all your help. To casino executive Cecil Fredi, my thanks for sharing your knowledge and becoming a friend in the process.

To Don Laughlin and Benny Binion, two Nevada pioneers, a special thank you. It says a lot for a man when he bares his soul to a writer — and I hope my words do justice to their pioneer spirit. Thanks to Bobby Baucom, for arranging my schedule at the Dunes so that I could write this book; to other friends and co-workers for their support; to Jim Snape and Ron Dewey, for distributing kindness as well as books; and to my wife who will once again see what I look like without glasses on.

And most importantly, my thanks to you — for sharing a few hours in Las Vegas, Behind The Tables.

Barney Vinson

LAS VEGAS
BEHIND THE TABLES!
PART 2

From the Author...

It was over twenty years ago when I first rolled into Las Vegas, on a scorching July afternoon. The town was spread out like an overturned pirate's chest in the middle of a sea of sand, the hotels great big dominoes washed in light. The thing I remember most, though, was walking into a Vegas casino for the very first time. Suddenly the heat and everything else quit being important.

I had stepped over into another world, one crammed full of noise and lights and people and excitement. There was a constant hum in the air, resembling the dull drone of a beehive. I could hear the rumble of a thousand discarded conversations, electronic buzzers going off, someone being paged, a stickman saying "winner seven" way in the background, and the sound of money. Money usually whispers, but you can still hear it in the slot machines. It comes clanging out into those metal trays, and it gets your attention in a hurry.

I had never seen so many girls. They were like pastel watercolors, with nice tans and straight teeth and eyes as big as silver dollars. When one smiled at you, you wanted to chuck your job and take her off to Mexico. They all wore hose and their legs were perfect, and the only thing different was what they sold: cigarettes, lighted yoyos, cocktail rings, Singapore Slings, all night flings, crazy things.

So there I was in Las Vegas. Like I said, the people were everywhere, and they were all betting their money on something. I started edging through the crowd, nonchalantly trying to ease my wallet out, trying to remember how much money I had without counting it in public. With all those people, there had to be a few crooks around.

My mind was spinning, just like the little ball on the roulette wheel. That made me start thinking about "Viva Las Vegas" and Elvis, the rat pack and Mister Sinatra, even Humphrey Bogart and Rick's nightclub in Casablanca. "Let it ride," Bogie would say with that lispish sneer. The action was always at the roulette wheel in the movies, but it all looked kind of dumb to me.

"Hi hon, could I get you a beer?"

"Heineken if you have it... Oh, you only have Miller Lite on tap? Thanks, I'll just go to the bar... Excuse me, please... Excuse me."

I never saw so many people in one room in my life. I like the way they just stop, right in the middle of the aisle, and stare straight up at the ceiling.

"Hey lady, what are you looking at? The action's down here!"

Do you know what I like about Las Vegas? It makes you feel like somebody else for a little while. You forget about alimony payments and stock options, and sales quotas, and leaky faucets. All you need are a few dollars in your pocket and an itch to be a kid again. Speaking of money, it's time I took a quick accounting. Let's see, there's two-seventy-five in cash, another hundred hidden behind my driver's license, almost four hundred... plus two thousand on my Visa... time to put up or shut up.

The craps tables loom ahead, and I can't help myself.

"Hello, could I get ten dollars worth of quarters?"

"Sorry, buddy, this is a five dollar game."

Great, now everyone is staring at me. "Okay," I hear myself saying, "give me five dollars on eleven."

"You got a bet, mister."

Come on, you beautiful babies, get me an eleven and I'll kiss your spots off. Come on, come on —

"Yo-leven!"

I won? I don't believe it. "Let it ride." What am I *doing?*

"YO-LEVEN!"

I stand there in a daze, it happened so fast. Are those one hundred dollar chips? God, they're only plastic. I throw a tip to the dealers and start to walk away. Just then a guy in a gray pinstripe stops me. I give him a quick onceover. He's not young, not old, the sort of fellow you wouldn't remember in a crowd. Red tie, matching handkerchief, a bulge under his coat. That wouldn't be a gun, would it? He flashes a smile, and I relax.

"My card," he says, the lights bouncing off ten gleaming fingernails. He wants me to be the hotel's guest for dinner, and he wants my name. "Bogart," I grin, and aim for the bar. Talk makes me thirsty.

There is an empty table near the small stage, and I order a drink. The cocktail waitress smells like flowers, but her eyes are light-years away. Alone again, I splash the chips on the table and count up. Nine blacks, five greens... a thousand and twenty-five dollars! I feel the blood surging to my head, and I am almost out of my seat and headed back for the dice table when the music starts.

She is at the piano, playing a song I cannot quite recall, and just when I am wondering what her voice sounds like she begins to sing. The best way to describe it, I guess, is like melted chocolate, kind of husky but so feminine that my skin tingles. A solitary spotlight trains on her face. My heart beats faster. I remember her from somewhere else, but like the song it won't come back.

Then her eyes catch on mine, and up rush all those tender times from a million years ago . . . the senior prom, my old Chevy, holding her close; the moment notched in time when we promised to wait forever but never waited at all. I whisper her name, and then the music is over. I am back at the front door, just coming in out of the heat.

Maybe it was just a dream, I don't know. Perhaps it was an omen of things to come, if such is possible. I do know that dreams have a way of coming true in Las Vegas. I've seen it happen, and it is part of the magic.

I will always have a special spot in my heart for this crazy noisy place, and all those Damon Runyan characters I had the pleasure to meet. I hope by sharing these pages and memories with you that Las Vegas will be more than just a jumble of neon and come-on. It is, after all, a little bit different from all the rest.

There is an old saw that locals love to spout: "Come here with money and leave on the bus. But come here with nothing, and linger with us."

I cherish the zany anecdotes and the sheer bravado of the warriors behind the tables . . . the cocktail waitresses and the dealers, the bartenders and the cashiers, and even the pit bosses with the tattered superstitions that will get them through another shift. They could have bought land when it was $100 an acre, but they didn't. They could have retired ten years ago, if they had saved their money. They could go somewhere else and get a better job, but they won't.

These are the people who really wrote this book, and I thank them one and all.

— Barney Vinson

To Bobby and Sue Young
who said, "Yes you can,"
and to Debbie Vinson
who said, "Yes I will."

CHAPTER 1

Chain Of Command

Each Las Vegas resort is like a city within a city. Its mayor is the corporation president, its city council the corporation's board of directors. The police chief is the casino manager, and his deputies include the various shift bosses and pit bosses who patrol the casino like old battered tiger sharks. Then come all the rest: the floor personnel, dealers, cocktail waitresses, hosts, pit clerks, chip runners, security guards, and on and on. It is no wonder that an average Las Vegas resort employs upwards of 2,000 people.

The tourist sees a casino...row upon row of jangling slot machines, blackjack tables that stretch into infinity, dusty chandeliers that sprinkle the room with muted light, dealers who deftly arch cards, retrieve dice, spin balls, and scoop up chips in small liquid movements. What the tourist does not see is another story.

Memos filter down from management with unerring regularity. For every "do" there is a "do not." Employees are told where to eat (and not to eat), where to park (and not to park), where to relieve one's self, and on occasion *when* to relieve one's self. A dealer once whispered to the floorman that he had to leave the table.

1

"I've got to go to the bathroom," he said under his breath. The floorman regarded him with baleful eyes. Finally he asked the dealer in a loud ringing voice, "Do you have to do number one, or number two?"

To the novice tourist, however, anything out of the ordinary in Las Vegas is of major consequence. Imagine a Vegas first-timer at the table, overhearing such a conversation, and then muttering to a friend, "Something big is happening. The dealer just told that guy in the suit that he's going to do a 'number two.' " "Did you hear that, Sam? One of the dealers is doing a 'number two.' " Sam: "Must be some kind of code. Get Charley." Charley: "A 'number two,' huh? Something's coming down. They're probably putting in loaded dice or something."

By the time Sam and Charley get back to Iowa, the story will have launched another Las Vegas legend. A certain casino in town is "two-timing" the public, and they saw it happen! And it must have worked, because when the dealer came back to the table he had a big smile on his face.

In the opinion of many, the dealer is the most important person in the casino industry. Why? Because he is the direct link between the resort and the customer. If a dealer is courteous and friendly, the player will be encouraged to gamble until — "Excuse me, is there a bank around here anywhere?" If a dealer is surly or rude, the player is intimidated and will go someplace else. A woman customer once asked a dealer, "Where are you from?" The dealer looked up as she shuffled her cards and said, "What difference does it make where I'm from?" A woman asked another dealer if he remembered her from the day before. He answered, "No, but I remember the dress."

Then again, being a dealer in Vegas is one of the most overrated and underpaid jobs in America. (Average salary:

$27 a day plus tips.) It sounds like a glamorous way to make a living, but eight hours of seeing people lose their money, their temper, and drink themselves into oblivion is enough to send anyone to the monkey house. A blackjack dealer in one casino made a six-card 21, only to find himself looking into the mottled face of one of the players. "You dirty son of a bitch," the player roared. The dealer spread the cards (official procedure), clapped his hands (official procedure) and whacked the player right in the chops (unofficial procedure).

A blackjack dealer found himself with three slow customers at his game, and one impatient player who kept scratching for a card even though he was at the last spot on the table. By the time the dealer got to the last man, he was gone — and so were his chips *and* his cards! Not to worry. The dealer looked around the casino, and there was his player. . .at another blackjack table holding his same two cards. And when the player scratched for another card, the dealer gave him one!

At one time, dealers were not permitted to talk to the players; it was too much like hustling. When a dealer got a tip, that money was out of the casino's grasp forever. Then in the late '70s a deluge of hotels — and the advent of legalized gambling in Atlantic City — caused gaming bosses to completely reverse this policy. Suddenly it was all right to speak to the customers, to say "good morning" and "good evening" and "good luck." Today, each hotel posts rules and regulations stressing the importance of being friendly — with thinly veiled threats of termination for offenders. Our only concern is exactly how the word "termination" is defined. Does it mean "dismissal" or does it mean what it meant when Stalin purged Russia? The list that follows comes from the current handbook of one Las

Vegas Strip casino. The dealers who work there are lucky; there were only 45 ways they could get (choke) "terminated."

RULE VIOLATIONS

1. Falsifying personnel or company records.
2. Insubordination — failure to follow a supervisor's direct order.
3. Rudeness or discourteous treatment of a Hotel guest or fellow employee.
4. Dishonesty or failure to follow cash handling procedures.
5. Removing any Hotel property or property of a guest or another employee, including food, liquor, soda, etc., from the premises without written permission from the department head.
6. No employee will give any other employee any Hotel property or merchandise including food and beverage without proper written authorization.
7. Wrongful possession, use, sale or transfer, of any alcoholic beverage, or controlled substance on Hotel premises.
8. Being under the influence of alcohol or controlled substance on Company property.
9. Sleeping on the job.
10. No on the job visitor or personal telephone calls (except emergency).
11. Taking more than specified time for meals or rest periods.
12. Productivity and/or workmanship not up to Dunes standards.
13. Being absent from work without notifying department head, shift manager or Time Office, as required.
14. Failing to call at least four (4) hours prior to the start of the shift to report an absence or late arrival.
15. Habitual tardiness or absenteeism (3 times in a 30 day period).
16. You must physically present yourself at the Time Office to punch in and out. All employees must punch out immediately following the end of their shift.
17. Misusing, destroying or damaging Hotel property, property of a guest or fellow employees.
18. Making false, malicious or profane statements concerning another employee, a guest or customer, or the Hotel and its facilities.
19. Fighting during working hours or on Company premises at any time.

20. Engaging in horseplay, scuffling, throwing things, shouting or demonstrating.
21. Wasting time, loitering or leaving assigned work areas during working hours.
22. Creating or contributing to unsanitary, unsafe or poor housekeeping conditions.
23. Soliciting, procuring or engaging in any immoral act on the premises.
24. Soliciting fellow employees for the sale of items, or the distribution of literature in unauthorized areas.
25. Visiting Hotel rooms or unauthorized areas at any time when not required by your job, without the express premission of management.
26. Violation of a security/safety rule, procedure or practice, or failing to cooperate with a security officer in the performance of their duties.
27. Interfering with Hotel discipline or efficiency.
28. Unauthorized release of confidential information regarding the Hotel, employees, guests or customers.
29. Bringing to the premises or possessing on Hotel premises, weapons (including explosives), cameras or recording devices without written permission from the Department Head.
30. Posting, removing or altering any matter on bulletin boards without Management's approval.
31. Lending money to, or borrowing money from, guests or other employees.
32. Soliciting a gratuity or "toke" from a guest.
33. Obtaining extra or unauthorized meals.
34. Altering or defacing Hotel uniforms or badges.
35. Wearing a uniform off Hotel premises without supervisor's approval.
36. Wearing a uniform off Hotel premises when off-duty, except directly to and from work.
37. Failing to return on the specified date from an approved leave of absence.
38. Accepting outside employment while on a leave of absence without written approval from the President.
39. Smoking in "No Smoking" areas.
40. Assignment of wages or frequent garnishments.
41. Exceeding the speed limit or driving or parking improperly on Hotel premises.

42. Engaging in any activity prohibited by Law shall be grounds for immediate dismissal.
43. Employees are not to gamble at any time on Company premises.
44. Not being on your assigned work station at the beginning and end of your shift.

Dealers must also have a valid Sheriff's card before starting a job, and must renew it prior to the card's expiration date (this doesn't mean they've been deputized; it just means they've been "checked out"). "Failure to do so may be subject to disciplinary action up to and including discharge/termination." Many casinos now have alcohol and drug testing policies. "Failure to agree to submit to the test or failure to provide an adequate explanation for the test results will result in the employee's immediate termination." The dealer's job comes before anything else, of course, and if there is any conflict of interest this must be reported to one's supervisor. "Failure to do so will result in disciplinary action up to and including termination."

Polygraphs? "If a situation occurs that causes Management to believe that a polygraph examination is necessary and appropriate, you will be asked to submit to testing. Failure to do so will result in . . . termination."

Inside the casino, dealers are on the same prestige level as cocktail waitresses, cage personnel and security guards. Social interaction is complex, and the pecking order breaks down like this:

Casino owner — casino manager — shift boss — pit boss — floorman — dealer.

It is almost like being in the army, where the chain of command would be along this line:

General — colonel — major — captain — sergeant — buck private.

Dealers themselves are classified and ranked according to the particular game they deal, which complicates the social structure even more:

Baccarat dealer — craps dealer — blackjack dealer — roulette dealer — Big 6 dealer — poker dealer.

Baccarat dealers get to wear tuxedos with red hankies in the pockets; craps dealers and blackjack dealers wear black pants and white shirts; poker dealers have their own dress code because they usually work for someone who is leasing the card room. They may even roll up their sleeves (if they happen to be wearing shirts at all).

Since dealers do not make the big money they once did, they are less likely to be browbeaten by floormen and pit bosses. One dealer was chastised by a pit boss for dealing with his shoes off. The dealer interrupted him. "Who's the president of the United States?" he said to the pit boss. "What difference does that make?" the pit boss blinked. "Who's the president of the United States?" repeated the dealer. The pit boss, flustered by this time, finally answered, "Uhh, Ronald Reagan." The dealer said, "Well, go tell Ronald Reagan for all I care."

A dealer was once accused of cheating because he idly rubbed his nose while dealing a hand of blackjack. "I saw what you did," the pit boss cried. "You were telling the players that you had a ten in the hole! I know every crooked move there is, and that's one of the oldest." The same pit boss was notorious for switching dealers when the pit was losing, and for transferring "unlucky" dealers from one shift to another. He also had the unnerving habit of kicking a metal wastebasket every time a dealer lost a hand.

The Gaming Control Board notes, however, that such procedures are standard practice in most casinos. "Many casino people are superstitious and will change dealers or close a particular table if someone is winning a considerable amount of money." It just makes sense to put the lucky dealers on the $5 and $25 games, and the unlucky dealers on the $1 games. That way, the casino does not lose as much money, and Lady Luck is foiled again. "We lost fifteen thousand on Table Six, boss, but I took the dealer off and put her on the game in the corner. She can't hurt us now."

Basically, the job of the dealer is fairly simple to define. He (or she) deals the game, sells chips to customers, takes losing bets and pays winning bets. He has the patience of a tortoise, the courage of an eagle, the agility of a mountain goat and the peripheral vision of an octopus. This enables the dealer to guard against cheaters, and to also watch for — *the floorman*. Such moves as looking under one's armpit while standing stationary would be a matter of great concern to a doctor or chiropractor, but relax gentlemen, the dealer is merely getting ready to pounce on another unsuspecting player. It may never be shown on "Wild Kingdom," where one antelope is chased to its doom by a dozen wild dingos. In Las Vegas, all it takes is one intoxicated gambler, one occupied floorman, and one hungry dealer with a payment due on his motorhome.

During a busy holiday weekend, a craps dealer leaned over and said to a player, "Don't forget the hard way." This particular player had been making hard way bets for the dealers all day, so he tossed a $5 chip to the stickman.

The floorman was lurking immediately behind the dealer, and it was one of those rare instances when the dealer did not detect the floorman's presence. "What did you just ask that player?" the floorman howled. The dealer, thinking fast, replied, "I, ah, asked him. . .if he was going to be here for the holiday."

The floorman's job is to protect the bankroll at all costs. If the chips on the table go down, so does the floorman's prestige. Consequently, he has to be prepared for such eventualities by rehearsing the following speech until he can say it in his sleep (which is usually while he is watching the game): "I never saw anything like it. The dice just went crazy." For this the floorman gets around $150 a day, business cards with his name on them, and all the cokes he can badger from the cocktail waitress. The floorman settles disputes between the dealers and the players, supervises payoffs and fills, signs markers, evaluates players, and is constantly on the lookout for — *the pit boss.* (The casino calls a grouping of tables a "pit," hence the term, "Pit Boss.")

Pit bosses have been the butt of many "inside" jokes over the years, for a host of reasons, not the least of which is the fact that they are. . .bosses. These guys have been known to antagonize a player or two, a dealer or two, and up pops another story. The bosses are thought by some to have a boring, do-nothing job, and up pops another story.

The Rabbit and the Snake

A blind rabbit happened upon a blind snake in the forest. "Let me touch you," the blind snake said, "so I can tell what kind of animal you are." "Uhh, okay," said the rabbit.

The snake felt the rabbit and then announced, "You are fluffy, and you have long ears, and you have a tail — so you must be a rabbit."

"Very good," said the rabbit. "Now it's my turn." He felt the snake, and then he said, "Well, you are cold, and slimy, and you don't have any balls — so you must be a *pit boss!*"

The pit boss is responsible for the operation of the entire pit. As a rule, he has a great deal of experience in supervising others such as being an ex-drill instructor in the Marine Corps or a lion-tamer for Ringling Brothers. The pit boss is in charge of scheduling the employees for each shift, settling disputes between the floormen and the dealers, and keeping a sufficient amount of chips on each game. When a game runs low on chips, the pit boss will grudgingly order a fill from the cashier's cage.

Nevada Gaming Commission Regulation 6.240 specifies the procedure for handling a fill. "All fill slips requesting chips or money must be prepared in triplicate at the time a fill is made . . . and then shall be hand carried from the cashier's cage, along with the fill." Five signatures are required before the process is completed, including those of the cashier, the chip runner, the pit boss, the floorman, and either the dealer at the blackjack table or the boxman (table supervisor) at the craps table. Afterwards, the three fill slips, dated and time-stamped, are distributed in the following manner:

The original goes into the drop box on the table. The first carbon copy stays at the cashier's cage. The second carbon copy remains in a locked box in the pit. Eventually, all copies wind up in the accounting department, where they are checked against the pit record. This procedure wears out a lot of ballpoint pens, but the reason for it is obvious. Forging fill slips was a favorite ploy of disreputable casino operators before such controls were instituted. It was easy to make out a fill slip for a large sum of money, erase a few zeros on the way to the table, and go home about thirty pounds overweight.

Today's record-keeping chores cause more delays than an airplane flight to Mexico. Auditing controls have to satisfy not only the Gaming Control Board, but the IRS ...the SEC...and the CPAs who inspect the IBMs for the hotel's VIPs. One casino cage manager said that 45 different complex forms had to be filled out each day just for various regulatory agencies. This includes such dire-sounding documents as the shift inventory transfer sheet, the working stiff sheet, the final stiff sheet, and the hit sheet...all of which are enough to make somebody try to hang himself with a *bed* sheet.

The hit sheet itemizes the winnings or losses of individual players in each pit. Instead of a Who's Who, this is more like a Who *Was*. Cash players are entered as C/P, and gamblers who take markers are listed by name. The pit clerk usually has the responsibility of making up the hit sheet. She also enters markers and payments in the computer, gives credit information to the floormen on players requesting markers, keeps the pit area stocked with rating cards and other supplies, makes showroom and dinner reservations for customers, and answers the phone. In other words, the pit clerk does *everything*. Without pit clerks, all floormen and pit bosses would fly into walls like blinded bats with their radar jammed, thrashing in chaos until their pinky rings fell off.

For instance, just answering the telephone in a Vegas casino can be an adventure. ''Yes, I'm calling from

Montgomery, Alabamuh. We got us a little argument going here, and I thought maybe you could settle it for us. In that game of blackjack, does the player make his bet before he sees his cards, or does he get to look at his cards first? I mean, I been playing poker all my life, and I just can't believe somebody'd be dumb enough to play a game where he has to make his bet before he sees what he's got. What's that? Are you *sure* about that, ma'am? Well, thank you kindly anyhow.''

One pit clerk had a memorable experience. ''About five years ago, a player from Hong Kong came in late Friday afternoon. He sat down at a blackjack table, and did not leave his chair until Monday morning. We even had his meals served at the game. When he left, he'd lost half a million dollars.''

Overseeing the dealers, floormen, pit bosses and pit clerks is — *the shift boss*. He can be identified by a cauliflower ear, which he acquired from spending seven hours a day on the telephone. The jobs of the shift boss are as varied as the patterns on his sports jacket. He is in charge of all table games, enforces casino policy, authorizes payoffs on winning keno tickets and slot machine jackpots, and spends the rest of his time dodging customers who are in pursuit of free rooms and free meals. He can usually be found eating prime rib in the coffee shop with — *the casino manager*.

The casino manager handles such day-to-day duties as monitoring and promoting business, authorizing credit, and greeting the customers who slipped past the shift boss. This is where the computer comes in handy. ''It would be impossible for me to remember every customer who walks through the door,'' one casino manager said. ''Obviously, it only takes me a few seconds to reestablish in my mind exactly what kind of customer he is, because once I say hello to him he is going to ask me for something. In this day and age, we try to give a deserving player everything he is entitled to, and then some. But we can't give the hotel away. The computer is a guideline that indicates exactly what I can do for each customer.''

Another task of the casino manager is to read the daily profit-and-loss statement prepared by the accounting department, and to take appropriate measures when the casino's hold* goes down on any of the games. ''What happened to Table Six last night?'' ''The cards went bad.'' ''What happened to Table One?'' ''The dice went bad.'' ''Okay, change the cards, change the dice, and — phew — change your after shave.''

Before becoming General Manager of the Stardust, Joe Viscuglia was the hotel's casino manager. He says, ''The hardest part of running a casino is dealing with customers and employees. These casino managers that come out of college, their knowledge is all theoretical. A guy who runs a good joint should be seen in the joint. That's what made Sam Boyd, Jackie Gaughan and Benny Binion great. They sat with their customers and employees in the casino. They didn't have an ivory tower syndrome.''

Well said.

Viscuglia began his career as a shill, and then went on to become a dealer, a shift boss, and a casino manager.

---

*There are three words by which each casino is governed: the *handle*, the *hold*, and the *drop*. The term ''handle'' refers to the total value of all the wagers a customer makes. The ''drop'' is the amount of money and markers ''dropped'' on each game (a measure of the players' ''stake'' in the game). The ''hold'' is the percentage of the drop that the casino wins. Simply stated, if the Hold for a particular game is 20 percent, then the casino expects to keep $20 out of every $100 dropped (not to be confused with the game's actual percentage, such as 5.26% for roulette).

It was more or less the same story for Casino Executive Jay Love. He started as a student dealer downtown, then dealt at such glamorous resorts as the Dunes, Stardust, and Caesars Palace. At Caesars, he worked his way up from dealer to shift boss, and later returned to the Dunes as a shift boss before being named casino manager.

Love says he spends half his working day going over records and statistics. "Without it, you couldn't really manage one of these places. Obviously, we keep the percentages on all the games. What I look for as a casino manager is something that stays irregular. None of these games is going to lose for a long period of time. If this does happen, we convince the management of the hotel that it will turn around. . .and 99 percent of the time it does."

The casino manager also sets the policy on how the games in each pit are dealt. That does not mean he can change the rules.

Major changes have to be submitted to the Gaming Control Board for an official okay, and approval would not be forthcoming if the changes altered the odds to the point where nobody ever won anything. After all, it would not be fair to the player if he were fined $500 for throwing the dice off the craps table. . .or if he were paid quadruple for a blackjack and every other hand was an automatic loser.

The casino manager, however, might decide to change the way the cards are dealt at the blackjack tables. There was a time, for instance, when the cards were dealt face-down out of a single deck. Then a casino manager came up with the idea of using a shoe holding multiple decks of playing cards. . .to deter card counters. Another casino manager came up with the idea of having the cards dealt face-up (except the dealer's first card). . .to deter cheaters by preventing them from touching the cards. Yet another casino manager thought of the idea of using automatic shufflers to deter slowpokes and really stymie card counters. The game has become so regimented that the players do not even have to *be* there. As a matter of fact, there was a blackjack fanatic from Texas who used to call his favorite Vegas casino several times a month. "Deal me a hand for five hundred," he would tell the pit boss on the telephone. If he lost, he would send a check in the mail. If he won. . .hmm, come to think about it, he never did.

One casino manager instituted a confusing policy of not allowing his blackjack dealers to peek at their unexposed "hole" card when they had a ten-count card showing. The casino manager figured that if the dealer did not look at his bottom card he would not accidentally expose it to the players, or intentionally signal its value to a confederate at the table. If the hand ended with the dealer having a blackjack, the players only lost their original bets if they split pairs or doubled down, but players who had *drawn* to 21 would lose. Consequently, the dealer spent half his time dealing the game and half his time trying to explain what the hell was going on.

There was the time a young man motioned for an extra card and wound up with 21. Sure enough, the dealer turned over a blackjack and took his money. "Wait," cried the young man, "I had 21." Recited the dealer, "Yes, but I had a blackjack, so you have to lose." In fact, this dealer used the same memorized speech so often that she finally goofed it up. When another player questioned her after his chips disappeared, she said, "I had a blackjack, so you have to leave." Before the dealer could correct herself, the player stood and headed for the front door. "Rules are rules," he was probably thinking.

The biggest headache faced by a casino manager is

approving complimentaries for hotel players. "The business has changed," Jay Love admits. "Today everybody is worried about comps. Everybody is comp-conscious. They feel unless a guy proves himself, he doesn't deserve anything." In Love's opinion, the average $5,000 customer is the one who has suffered. "This kind of customer comes in four or five times a year, and ends up blowing $15,000 or $20,000. That's a pretty darn good customer. I think the high customer still gets comped to what he should, but it's that mediocre customer . . . who has been the backbone of this city for 40 years . . . that is being neglected."

Pleasing the customer is the only way a casino can be successful, Love says. "Regardless of what anyone has told you about the gambling business, the correct term for it is a 'people' business. It's a challenge to make sure the customer leaves feeling that he enjoyed himself and will return."

This means coming up with a funny answer when a customer tries to get his gambling marker reduced for some off-the-wall reason. "I didn't have enough towels in my room, so take $1,000 off my marker." ('Oh, dry up!') "The faucet dripped in the bathroom all night, and I think I ought to get $2,000 off my marker." ('You're all wet!') Or: "The maid woke me up, so how about taking $3,000 off my marker?" ('I'll take the money, you take the maid.')

A marker is like a casino credit card. With marker privileges, a player can take money up to a pre-specified credit line set up by the cashier's cage. Without these privileges, a player can only take money up to the pre-specified credit line of his wallet. It may be pleasing to one's ego to walk up to a table and say, "Give me a thousand." Then hear the dealer say, "Yes *sir*," as he pushes tall stacks of chips across the table and other players look on with awe. But comes the day of reckoning, and: "How'd you want to pay that twenty grand, Mister V?" Gulp.

On occasion, however, it is possible to wiggle off the hook. "I've had cases where people felt they had already paid their marker," Love said. "I've even had to call Gaming Control and take the box off the game in the middle of a shift, which is a no-no, and show the customer his marker stub. In extreme instances, when I feel a customer is adamant that he is right, I invariably will give him his money back to show that we're not trying to do anything but have the best customer relationship we can have."

An Oriental player would bet only $500 chips when he played blackjack, and once accumulated $2,000 in $25 chips from odd payoffs during four hours at the table. The player went to the bathroom, leaving his chips behind. When he returned, he accused the casino of switching his $500 chips for the ones in front of him, saying there was no way he could have amassed that many $25 chips. The casino manager was called. "After listening to the customer, even though it was in broken English, I understood enough to know that he truly believed in his heart that somebody had switched his chips. I had the dealer count out $20,000 in $500 chips, gave him that, and took back the two stacks of $25 chips. It was a turnaround of $19,000." Here came the hotel president. "You're out of your mind," he told the casino manager. The player, meanwhile, was so happy about his new-found wealth that he decided to keep gambling, and by the end of the shift had lost close to $600,000. Here came the hotel president. "You're a genius," he told the casino manager.

The day is almost over. The hotel president goes back

to his office. The casino manager breathes a sigh of relief. The shift boss smiles sympathetically. A phone rings, and the pit clerk reaches wearily for the hit sheet. On the casino floor, the dealers are busy at work. "Money plays" on Table Four, "One down" on Table Two, "Blacks in action" on Table Three.

In the break room, one rumor dies and two new ones are born. Somebody complains about the IRS, and a cocktail waitress checks her lipstick in a hazy mirror. "Who's got the tokes?" one dealer asks another, while a floorman idly scans the want ads in the local paper. A two-bit poker game is going on at the card table.

The platoon of fresh GIs heads for the pit, and wristwatches are double-checked. The strength of the enemy is gauged, and the invasion begins. "Phillips, take out Gerardi. Wallace, you get Kaufman. Barnett, take out Hagan. Boehm, take out Murphy. Wampler, get Hayes. Broyles, take out Martinez. . ."

The night is just beginning.

CHAPTER 2

Games People Play

*"There is a child in all of us,
straining to break away,
eager to fight the wind,
impatient to be at play."*

John Romero

Security guards stopped a customer in a Strip casino when they noticed he was "dispersing a white substance" from a container he was carrying. The guards figured they had captured a drug dealer, and took him into a back room for questioning. The man confessed, all right, but not to carrying cocaine. The white substance turned out to be the ashes of his Aunt Lucretia, whose final wish was that her remains be scattered in her favorite casino.

A drunk stumbled up to a "Big Bertha" slot machine and rifled through his pockets. He finally came out with a dollar token, and after three tries managed to get the coin into the slot. Sirens blared, and out cascaded a jackpot of $100! The drunk began stuffing the metal coins into his pants, but found himself reaching further and further for his pockets. It seems with all that added weight, his pants began to — gravitate.

A woman lost $200 in a Las Vegas slot machine and motioned to the change girl. "I need some more change," she declared. The change girl said, "Why don't you try another machine?" The woman answered, "Oh, I don't care if I win or not, honey. I just love to pull the handle."

A dealer once caught a player switching cards on a crowded blackjack game. He called the pit boss over. "This guy just made a switch," the dealer whispered to him. "If you want to grab him, you'll probably find a whole bunch of cards in his pocket." The other five players at the table watched in awe as the man was unceremoniously marched away by security guards. Finally, one said in a timid voice, "Boy, this isn't a very friendly hotel. When a player gets a blackjack, you people get all upset!"

An elderly woman was down to her last dollar on a downtown blackjack game. She was dealt 19, and the dealer had a face card showing. "Please don't have twenty," she said to the dealer. He peeked at his bottom card before dealing to the other players, then shook his head. "I'm not supposed to tell you this, but I *do* have twenty." With a shriek, the woman grabbed her dollar and ran from the table. Two security guards, standing nearby, saw the woman going out the door and took off in hot pursuit. They did not catch her, but the dealer never forgot the story. "I thought it was remarkable — these two big security guards chasing this old lady over a dollar."

One oldtimer remembers when a player lost $1,000 on the roulette wheel. This happened around six o'clock at night, just as the shifts were changing. The two shift bosses hated each other . . . and when the dealer started to put the money in the drop box, they nearly came to blows. Of course, the boss on day shift wanted the thousand in the day shift drop box, while the boss on swing shift wanted the money in *his* drop box. Soon a genuine tug-of-war was underway, each shift boss straining to yank the money from the other's hand. R-rr-rip. Two well-dressed casino executives went flying, each holding exactly one-half of ten $100 bills. The wrinkled-up, chewed-up, torn-up money was then swept up, split up, and put up. Half went into the day shift drop box, while the other half was deposited in the swing shift drop box. The auditing department later patched up the cash with Scotch tape. The two shift bosses never did patch up their differences.

A pit boss in another Strip hotel got so angry he shoved a floorman, whose table had just lost a considerable amount of money. The floorman retaliated by choking the pit boss with the latter's own necktie! This scenario unfolded the same day of the famous MGM Hotel fire, and many of the customers inside the casino had moved from the MGM to this nearby resort. After a harrowing day of seeing people rescued from a burning building by Air Force helicopters, they were now greeted with a wild west shootout that ended with security guards trying to break up the melee. The pit boss got in the last blow, while most of the customers were walking out of the hotel in disgust. He began hopping up and down on what he thought were the floorman's eyeglasses — which turned out to belong to one of the security guards. The guard was calling out, "Okay, break it up, you guys. Guys?"

In another casino, the pit boss harassed a dealer to the point where the dealer finally threw a punch at him in the dice pit. The pit boss, a former boxer in the Marine Corps, lifted the dealer off the floor and was about to send him on a one-way trip to the Promised Land. Unfortunately for the pit boss, there was a convention of professional wrestlers in the hotel at the time. Thinking an angry player was taking out his frustrations on a hapless dealer, the wrestler let out a war whoop and here he came. (And all this time we thought John Glenn was the first man in space.)

A burly man in a pair of shorts was shooting craps one night when a security guard noticed the man was showing more than public decency allowed. Since the guard's shift was almost over, he waited until his relief man arrived and told him about it. The new guard, a no-nonsense type, marched up to the man and said, "Reel yourself in," or words to that effect. The man was so embarassed he gave the security guard a $25 chip.

A rich gambler from Texas excused himself from the blackjack table to go to the men's room. When he returned, he was walking barefoot. "What happened to your boots?" asked the pit boss. "I gave the attendant a $500 chip to shine them for me," replied the wealthy (and somewhat inebriated) gambler. "Attendant?" the pit boss cried, "we don't have an attendant in the men's room!"

In the old days, the big game in Las Vegas was craps. Dunes operations boss Dennis Gomes explains. "Years ago, there were a lot of immigrants who had grown up in poor neighborhoods. They had played craps in the streets, and they were very familiar with the game. Suddenly they had money, and they were coming to Las Vegas. So at that point in time, the game of craps was at its peak of popularity.

"Now their kids are coming up, and they're not as familiar with the game. They're more affluent. They're more interested in 21 (blackjack). They've read all the books, and they think they can count cards. So 21 has gotten more popular as compared with the old man's game of craps."

Nevada casinos won a record $3.9 billion from gamblers

in 1987, and most of that money came from blackjack and slots players. A recent marketing report showed a total of 1,807 blackjack tables in Las Vegas, compared with 850 in Atlantic City. At the same time, there were 56,378 slot machines in Las Vegas casinos, and only 18,000 similar devices in Atlantic City. On the other hand, Atlantic City had 250 craps tables, compared with 245 in Las Vegas. Four New Jersey casinos boast 24 dice tables each, while in Las Vegas it is unusual to see more than half a dozen tables in any casino.

"We get a different type of player," an Atlantic City spokesman said. "We get city guys, people who are serious about gambling. In Las Vegas, you're talking about somebody on a holiday...someone that's just having fun."

Maybe so, but a retired Las Vegas casino executive once bet a friend $50 that the two of them could stand at a Vegas dice table for ten minutes and never see anyone laugh out loud. His friend took the bet. "Not only did we not see anyone laugh, we never even saw anybody smile. It was the easiest fifty I ever won."

The players never smile, because of stringent new policies concerning "comp" privileges. The cocktail waitress even has to get permission from the floorman before bringing cigarettes or bottled beer to a player. One man lost $500 at the dice table, and asked for a ticket to the buffet. The only person who could approve the request was the shift boss, and he was on vacation. The casino manager had to be located, while the player stood waiting for half an hour. Incidentally, the buffet in this particular casino was $3.50.

The dealers have not smiled much lately either. Their income from tips has dropped dramatically. Today, any dealer who does not declare all his tip income finds himself a member of the "endangered wildlife" species. In 1988, IRS agents raided the toke boxes at Caesars Palace, confiscating money owed by fifteen dealers. The hotel, in an effort to avoid such an incident in the future, forced the dealers to begin pooling their tips. In the past, tips had been divided among each four-man dice crew. Now that all the dealers are getting the same amount of money each day, the IRS knows exactly who is declaring all their income — and who is not.

Other Las Vegas resorts will no doubt follow suit, with dealers in one casino already being told to either settle their disputes with the IRS, or face suspension. In fact, the day is probably not too distant when taxes will be taken out of tip earnings before the dealers even receive the money. It has always been that way in Atlantic City.

And there is yet another reason why dealers and players aren't smiling. A few years ago, the government legalized an ominous bill called Regulation 6A. Whenever a player's transactions exceeded $10,000 in cash in a 24-hour period, his name and social security number went to the IRS. Suddenly, all the high rollers high-tailed it to the Caribbean, and there went most of the big scores Vegas dealers lived for. Big wins usually meant big tips.

There is another foreboding cloud on the horizon. Picture yourself in your favorite casino a few years ago, playing slots. Out of nickels? No problem, because there were change girls everywhere. But now they're harder and harder to find. They dispensed money, and they dispensed advice. "Try that one in the corner. No one's hit a jackpot on it all night, and it's ripe. Stay away from that one, dear. A woman hit it five minutes ago."

The Universal Slot Machine Company has developed a new electronic "bill validator" which attaches to each machine and converts paper money into coins, thereby doing away with the need for change personnel at all. The validator can change bills of any denomination, using a larger coin "hopper" that holds 3,000 coins. The beauty of it is that when a customer inserts a bill for change, the coins pour out in the same manner as a regular jackpot. Consequently, everyone thinks everyone else is winning a fortune, while all they are really doing is just getting more change! Circus Circus has already put in its bid for 10,000 of them.

Another device from Universal Slots is an electronic coin acceptor that can be programmed to detect and eject counterfeit coins, or "slugs." This invention could save Las Vegas casino operators up to $20 million a year in lost profits. The "brain" in Universal's new coin acceptor is a micoprocessor that scans for size, weight, composition and other coin characteristics programmed into memory. In a fraction of a second, it makes the decision to accept the coin, or send it thudding into the tray. Nickel alloy: okay. Brass alloy: okay. Lead: reject, reject, reject. Cecil Fredi, vice-president in charge of slots at the Dunes, says, "Nothing is going to revolutionize the industry such as these pieces of equipment."

Meanwhile, a cashless slot machine is being tested by another manufacturer that eliminates coins altogether. Bally says, "There will come a time when you'll give your money to a casino cashier, have it credited to your account and play with only a card." Games of Nevada has concocted something called a SLOTCOMM "On-Line" slot communication system, which consists of a communicator for each slot machine linked to a master computer. This system will make it easier to keep tabs on individual players, and "if effectively applied, could become the slot department's ultimate marketing tool.''

As late as 1967, table games were responsible for more than 80 percent of casino income in Las Vegas. ''Slot machines were in the casinos for one reason,'' Fredi said. ''To keep the wives happy while their husbands were at the tables. In percentages, a nickel machine was the same as a dollar machine.'' Each held between 15 and 20 percent, a return to the player of around 80 cents on the dollar.

As far as promotions were concerned, the creed by which slot managers lived in the early days was best summed up like so:

''You can fool some of the people all of the time, and all of the people some of the time...and that's good enough for me.''

In one casino, a slot machine boss came up with a meloncholy idea. ''I was driving down the Strip,'' one oldtimer recalled, ''and I see this old fella walking down the side of the road carrying a watermelon. Then a couple of blocks later I see another fella carrying a watermelon. I'm wondering what the hell's going on, and then I see someone coming out of this casino carrying a watermelon. I went inside, and there was a watermelon on top of every single slot machine in the joint — and a sign which said, 'With every watermelon jackpot, win a big prize!' ''

Another slot manager offered free personalized key chains just for coming inside. Of course, he just happened to be out of key chains with your name on them, ''but we'll have one made up right away.'' In the meantime, two slot machines set up on either side of the key chain booth were spitting out jackpots right and left. Since there were some empty machines nearby, and since the key chain would be ready any minute now — ''oh, what the heck, give me ten dollars in nickels. ''

"Hey, that's a nice key chain, Boob."

"That's supposed to say 'Bob.' And the damn thing cost me SEVENTY-FIVE DOLLARS!!''

How about this one? Get about 200 little plastic eggs, put a $2 bill inside each one, and have a drawing every night for all the jackpot winners. Of course, they have to stick around for the drawing which is: TONIGHT, 9 P.M. WIN ANYWHERE FROM $1 TO $100! Each winner dips his hand into the bowl and withdraws a plastic egg, while the slot manager shouts into the mike: "Get a dollar, get a dollar." The winner breaks into a grin as he reads he has won *two* dollars! He doesn't feel bad, because he is thinking how he stuck it to the guy who was hoping he would only win one dollar.

There is an old joke about the sign on a slot machine that read: "This machine out of order; please throw your money in the wastebasket.'' People played slot machines because they did not understand craps or blackjack. They could gamble at their own pace and not be intimidated by live casino action. It was fun, it was easy, and occasionally money even came out of them. The coin trays were made of heavy metal, deliberately screwed loosely to the machines, and when somebody hit a $25 jackpot it almost registered on the Richter scale.

"Then, in 1975, Bally came out with what we call the 'wide body,' '' Fredi recalled. "That was the first dollar machine with a five percent hold, the first 'loose' slot machine. It took people all these years to realize that five percent of a dollar is a helluva lot more than 20 percent of a nickel." The technical term for it is "volatility," a slot machine's ability to achieve its theoretical house win percentage over a given period of time.

Things have not been the same since. Today, dollar slot machines provide 21 percent of the state's gambling take, with quarter machines kicking in another 23 percent. In fact, almost 60 percent of Nevada casino profits are generated from what Fredi called these former "second-class citizens." At the Frontier Hotel, poker machines take in ten times more than the poker room. Casino operations boss Richard Schuetz adds, "We've taken out a pit that once had eight tables games and we're making more money than ever." Says Bally's assistant slot manager Charles Lombardo: "The take from table games is stagnant, craps is even down. Slot players are the gamblers of the future."

Because of volatility and new technology, slot machine profits in Nevada casinos are skyrocketing: $1.81 billion vs. $1.49 billion for table games in 1985; $1.95 billion vs. $1.49 billion for table games in 1986. Table games, even with all those blackjack tables, cannot compete. Table games require lots of dealers and floormen and pit bosses. Table games fluctuate, and sometimes they actually lose. Slot machines, on the other hand, are what you might call pre-set at the factory. Inside each machine today is an inch-long gadget called an EPROM computer chip, programmed to return *most* of the money that people put inside of it. All the casino needs is a good slot mechanic, and that little three percent hold on dollar machines keeps rolling in — and that two percent hold on $5 machines — and that one percent hold on $25 machines.

Don Laughlin of the Riverside Casino in Laughlin will lament that he loses $12,000 a day on food in his resort. But Laughlin has 1,000 slot machines scattered throughout his casino — giving him a profit of $150,000 a *day*. Consequently, even mighty Caesar has taken notice. "Get those grapes out of my face; I gotta *think*." Stately Caesars

Palace, regal trendsetter that it is, recently gave away half a million dollars in cash prizes (awards presented through 107th place) to — slot machine players? Caesars Palace? Hang-out of the high rollers? The shindig was hosted by that distinguished luminary of film and radio, Wolfman Jack, and officials said it was a howling success. How could such a thing happen? Why, James Bond would roll over in his Aston Martin.

Loose slots is what did it. "That's the single most important thing," Fredi said. "When I was at the Frontier, we held some focus studies and actually talked to slot players. We learned a tremendous amount from them. A slot player says basically that he knows he is not going to win. That's in the back of his mind. But he wants to win. Everybody wants to be a winner."

Slot machine players were asked the following question: "Which would you rather hit on a nickel slot — four $25 jackpots, or one $100 jackpot?" Fredi tells what happened. "Far and away, the answer was four $25 jackpots. It's the thrill of winning. Let's say the average slot player has a budget of $1,000, and he's going to Vegas for a three-day stay. He wants to be able to play the maximum amount of time, and a good slot player will play ten hours a day without a doubt. At the end of 30 hours of playing time, our casino has that $1,000." And the player has had three days of fun.

In other words, it is better to have 250 people win $1,000 (who stick it back into the machines) than to pay out $250,000 to a single winner (who goes out the door with it). One slot machine representantive laid it on the line. "In the slot industry, we're all building creative new ways for players to lose their money. But that's like shooting yourself in the foot. We say you should build machines that give people a winning experience, because that's the only way to stimulate growth in the market.''

Meanwhile, the job of the Gaming Control Board is made easier because the casinos wouldn't dare change their slot percentages. As board administration chief Harlan Elges said, ''If one casino has its slots paying back 96 cents on each dollar played, and the one next door pays back 98, I guarantee that within an hour the casino paying 96 cents will be empty. The word travels very fast, so we don't even check on the percentage of payout unless a casino advertises a particular level. The competition basically keeps things in line, whether the machines are electronic or mechanical.''

Las Vegas locals, for example, demand more of a return on their money than do tourists, who play for shorter periods of time. That is why the locals play video poker machines. ''When video poker first came out,'' Fredi said, ''the hold was figured at about six or seven percent. Today the hold is around two percent on the same pay schedule. The reason is that people have gotten smarter on how to play. They'll throw away a winning combination to go for the royal flush.'' It is the best bet in Las Vegas, but the player has to be street smart. Look for the poker machine that pays 9 coins for a full house, and 6 coins for a flush. Most machines on the Strip pay only 8 coins for a full house, and 5 for a flush. As Fredi said, ''Unlike the slot machine, which you can loosen or tighten, the only thing you can do to a poker machine is change the pay scale.''

Higher payoffs mean higher profits, and the Gold Coast Casino found that out in a hurry. The Las Vegas casino opened in late 1986, with video poker machines taking up 60 percent of its slot space. Today, 80 percent of the slots at the Gold Coast are poker machines. Slot manager Gary

Hunter says, "The proper ratio for the locals is really 85 percent, and we'll have that before much longer."

Cecil Fredi was a big game hunter before he came to Las Vegas. Today he tracks a different kind of animal. "Everybody's got to have something, that's my philosophy. Some people play golf, some people are into religion, I like the outdoors. The main object of slot players is to play slots." Fredi was instrumental in getting qualified slot players treated the same as other premium guests, back when it was a real honor to be invited to a New Year's Eve party or an anniversary celebration. "There was everything you can imagine...the finest foods, booze, entertainment, and it was all free. But many times people would come up and say, 'Cecil, is it all right if we go play the machines now?' It's nice, they like it, but their main interest is the slot machines."

The way one wealthy slot player from Mississippi put it: "I appreciate yall's efforts, and I understand what you're doin', but just don't bother me when I'm on them slot machines!"

At one time, slot machines were a way of life in Las Vegas laundromats, doughnut shops, movie theaters, bakeries, restaurants, service stations, professional offices, car washes, airports, bus depots, fast food places, liquor stores, grocery stores, discount stores, drug stores and convenience stores. In fact, they were just about everywhere except jewelry stores, poodle parlors, grade schools, trade schools, high schools and swimming pools. The Clark County Liquor and Gaming Licensing Board, however, recently stopped granting slot licenses in most of these establishments, presumably under pressure from resort owners.

Henceforth, slot machines will only be found in casinos,

gift shops, drug stores, grocery stores, convenience stores, liquor stores, airports, bars, restaurants and *existing* laundromats and doughnut shops. Laundromat owners contend that the new law will cost each future laundry about $28,800 a year in lost revenue, or roughly one-fourth of one's total business. In the meantime, since an existing laundromat can still have slot machines, the owner finds himself in an enviable position. The washers and dryers may not be worth much, but that "grandfather slot machine clause" changes everything. "For Sale. Laundromat. Building: $10,000. Equipment: $2,500,000. Contact Mr. Al (Shorty) Fedgwick, Care of Beverly Hills Hotel, Bungalow 7."

The simple reason why slot machines are taking over Las Vegas is because people are winning at them — or at least, they think they are. It is the same story with blackjack. All the books say that players can win at blackjack, as long as they follow certain strategies. Even if the strategies do not always work, the player has still learned something. From John Gollehon's book *All About Blackjack*:

"To my way of thinking, the hesitancy to play blackjack is merely a lacking of confidence." By reading and studying various texts, the player comes away with "confidence, discipline, and a desire to win!"

That is the problem with fading stars like keno and roulette. Nobody wins anything. Look at keno. The house has an edge of over 25 percent! If a player bet every possible combination on a 10-spot keno ticket at a dollar each, he would invest a total amount of $1,646,492,110,120. He would win back a total of $1,204,962,232,896. In other words, he still lost about 342 billion dollars! It would be rather amusing, however, just to see the look on the keno manager's face when told by a ticket writer: "Excuse me, but the gentleman at the counter wants to bet a trillion dollars on the next game.''

The main attraction to keno is the idea of winning a fortune for a minimal risk. As keno manager John Martie said, ''Where else can you bet three dollars to win fifty thousand?'' He went on to say, ''Most people don't play for the big money anyway. They play for the $1,500 net win, so they don't have to pay taxes on it.'' The most popular bets, he said, are the $1 six-spot ticket, the $3 five-spot, and the $100 two-spot...all of which pay $1,500.

The drawbacks to keno are numerous. Supplies are expensive, manpower is extensive, and the game is boring. Admittedly, it gives a diner something to do while he waits an hour and 45 minutes for his sandwich in the coffee shop. At least, it *seems* that long. Since there are no clocks in Las Vegas, it is hard to tell. The only wall decorations you see are those brightly-lit electric keno boards. That brings to mind the famous celebrity who complained that everyone was staring at him in the casino's restaurant. Then he happened to look overhead, and discovered he was sitting underneath — the keno board!

Even though winning the top keno prize of $50,000 is nine times more difficult than winning a lottery, casino people seem to think the game will always be in demand. They blame the game's loss of popularity on such things as keno lounges being hidden from public view. One casino manager said, ''It'll never fade out as long as they put it in front of the public's eye, but it's like anything else — if they hide it, it's not successful.'' Winning apparently has little to do with it. We asked one keno manager how many $50,000 tickets he had paid out since the top prize doubled from $25,000 in 1978. His answer was: ''None.''

Think about it. If a keno game is ''run'' every five

minutes, that is roughly 12 games an hour, or 288 a day. This becomes 105,120 games a year, multiplied by ten years (which is how long the keno manager had not paid any $50,000 winners): or a grand total of 1,051,200 games — WITHOUT ONE WINNER! No wonder the casinos hide the keno lounges; they're *ashamed* of themselves.

Keno has managed to survive, however, and so has roulette. Unlike craps and blackjack, the atmosphere at the roulette wheel is relaxed and almost soothing. Occasionally the croupier will send the ball spinning, and eventually it plops into one of 38 slots on the roulette wheel. It is the most popular game of chance in the entire civilized world. But it is not popular in Las Vegas.

In European casinos, there is one zero on the roulette wheel, and the house edge is 2.70 percent. In Las Vegas, there are two zeros on the roulette wheel. That hikes the house edge to 5.26 percent, or:

"Hey, what happened to all my chips?"

According to a study by the Las Vegas Convention and Visitors Authority, only two percent of all visitors to Las Vegas even play roulette anymore. In fact, the only game lower on the hit parade is baccarat, which attracts less than one percent of the gamblers.

Baccarat was first introduced to Las Vegas at the Dunes in 1959. The game was a novelty at first, but now every major casino has a baccarat pit. The house edge is a scant 1.15 percent, which makes baccarat one of the best bets in town. It is a game of pure chance, with no elements of strategy. In his book *All About Baccarat*, John Gollehon writes:

"Baccarat offers the player the best odds of any casino game when you consider all the bets. Indeed, baccarat is probably the best game for the player who doesn't want to take the time to develop a skill ... but wants a good shot for his money."

But baccarat, even with its cloak of continental charm, is facing extinction in Nevada casinos. The problem is that the game is expensive. Most casinos have a $20 minimum bet. As one pit boss said, "If we didn't have baccarat, we wouldn't be a full-service resort." Besides, it is the only place in the casino where all the floormen can make free long-distance phone calls on the WATTS line.

One of the biggest casino money-makers is "The Big Six," or wheel of fortune. This carnival game somehow sneaked into Las Vegas casinos years ago, and offers the player: fun, exhilaration, thrills, chills, and everything else except a chance to win anything. The house edge ranges from 11.1 percent on a 1-to-1 payoff, to a numbing 24 percent on the 40-to-1 payoff. Yet it is exciting, and that is what gives the game its appeal. Some casinos even employ professional actors to run the money wheels, but the cost in salary is apparently well worth it. One Strip hotel averaged a monthly profit of $12,000 on its Big Six wheel, for a "hold" of 55 percent. In other words, out of every $10 "invested," a customer could expect a one-time dividend check of $4.50. Where is E. F. Hutton when you need him?

For sports book bettors, dreams die hard. Most of us are either too old or in such sad repair that we can barely walk across a football field, much less run across it for the game-winning touchdown. The next best thing is betting on one's favorite team, of being able to watch a 3-hour contest on television with a vested interest in the outcome.

The books make most of their money on the vigorish from each wager, which amounts to a 4.5 percent house advantage. What matters then is volume. According to the Nevada Gaming Control Board, close to $1 billion was bet in the state's 65 licensed sports books in 1987, but the house take was only $35.3 million.

Sports betting is second in Las Vegas only to casino action, and that is the reason every resort of consequence must have its own book. Without one, the sports bettor will make his bets somewhere else . . . and another chair at the blackjack table stays empty.

People who bet on sporting events are assured of two things if they give their business to casino sports books. One: Sophisticated technology (including three-dimensional screens in the near future) makes losing your money a lot more fun. Two: The New Orleans Saints will only win a football game when you bet against them.

CHAPTER 3

Winners and Losers

Terry Williams pushes three dollar tokens into the yawning mouth of the Megabucks slot machine. He is down $47, and has just called to a change girl for another fifty bucks in dollars.

"I remember seeing the first 7 drop; I remember seeing the second 7 drop; then the third 7 dropped and I thought to myself, 'Oh my God, I've got $15,000.' Of course, the fourth 7 was there, in front of my eyes, but I wasn't focused on it. When I finally saw the fourth 7, and we're talking micro-seconds, I knew immediately that I had won over four million dollars. I started yelling, and I knew I had to move. I felt like if I didn't I was going to explode. It was a feeling of power. I can't explain it, it was just a feeling that I had won. I kept saying over and over to myself, 'I did it, I did it, I did it.' It was sweet insanity, as if my entire world collapsed within me...and I don't know what that was. It came out of a primal part of myself, I think, of a caveman shoving a spear into a mastodon, and the mastodon falling. That was little old me playing against the odds that I knew were astronomical ...and I had done it, I had beaten them, I had *won*! I was bursting with pride, and I was bursting with power. I knew what it was like to be crazy."

Terry Williams had just won $4,988,842.14.

There was a program on televison a few years back called "The Millionaire," where an eccentric rich man named Tipton would give some poor struggling person a new chance in life with a check for a million dollars. The show was a hit, but it would not even raise eyebrows in these times, not when million dollar jackpots in Las Vegas are so commonplace that the news is relegated to the entertainment sections in the local newspapers.

Money Magazine recently polled 2,250 households, asking "What would you do if you suddenly came into a million dollars?" The answers were surprising. Eight out of ten Americans would keep on working, and half of those would stay at the same job. Is that a slap in the face with a wet sock, or what? What has happened to the Dagwood Bumsteads, the Dirty Harry Callahans, the Diamond Jim Bradys? It seems the salt of the earth has been replaced with Morton's Low-Sodium Lite Salt Substitute.

In the old days, winning a million in Las Vegas was nothing more than a pipe dream. Jackpots peaked on the slots at a hundred dollars, although it sounded like a lot more when the sirens started going off. Playing keno was the only way to win the big money, back when the top prize was just $25,000.

Whenever somebody won it back then, two things would happen: the lucky winner would get his picture in the paper and there would be a widespread investigation by the casino owner to find out how it happened. Sure enough, a man playing keno at a casino on the Strip circled eight of the 20 numbers that came up in the next game. "I won, I won," he cried, racing to the window. The owner of the casino, a respected businessman who has since passed on and had half the town named after him, ordered the man to undergo a lie detector test to prove he had not cheated. The man passed the test. The owner had the man take another, which he also passed. A third test was ordered, and this time the operator said, "Well, I didn't like the way he answered question number three..." That was what the casino owner was waiting for. The winner never got paid.

As this goes to print, the world record win on a Nevada slot machine is $6.8 million won by Cammie Brewer in 1988. Brewer lined up four 7's on a Megabucks progressive slot at Reno's Cal Neva Club on February 14th. "This settled my wife down," he said afterwards. It seemed old Cammie had forgotten to get her a Valentine's Day card.

The only trouble with sticking dollar tokens in a Megabucks slot machine is that it is almost impossible to stop doing it once you start. There is a computerized sign just overhead that constantly blinks out the giant jackpot, and the numbers change within fractions of each second, spiraling higher and higher. This reporter is an eyewitness to that, watching the pot jump from $5,450,611.85 to $5,451,312.25 within the space of twenty minutes while said reporter proceeded to lose $40 in that same period of time (never to be reimbursed by his publisher).

The attraction of Megabucks is that if the player lines up four jackpot symbols with only one dollar invested, the return is a mere $5,000. With two coins the jackpot is $10,000. The million dollar bonanza is good only if *three* dollar tokens are used. Consequently, it would be understandable to see a player deposit one lowly dollar token, if that was all he had left, and then actually pray that he would lose. It is nothing more than greed feeding on greed, and that is what keeps Megabucks going. The way one slot addict put it, the ash on her cigarette three inches long, "If you're gonna go, honey, you might as well go for the big stuff."

Megabucks was conceived as "logical competition" to the huge lottery jackpots operated by a number of states including California. International Game Technology (IGT) designed a network of slot machines placed in strategic casinos throughout Nevada, and linked to a single computer at their headquarters in Reno. The likelihood of lining up four Megabucks symbols is somewhere in the cosmos between Jupiter and Mars, and even a spokesman at IGT would not admit to the mathematical probability of hitting one of the blasted things. His comment was, "You've got a better chance of winning the Megabucks jackpot than you do of winning a state lottery." When put in those words it almost seems as though they are *giving* the money away, so it doesn't make much sense when they say an eventual Megabucks jackpot could go as high as fifteen million dollars.

Meanwhile, other progressive dollar slot machines are spewing out millionaires like popcorn. A Detroit housewife recently won $2.5 million at Caesars Palace on a progressive dollar slot, and three months later a Phoenix college student collected one million dollars just from "pumping iron." What makes it all so nice and believable is knowing that if this can happen to someone else, it can just as easily happen to us.

Take 24-year-old Lorraine Page. She was married in a Vegas wedding chapel one Easter weekend, and celebrated by playing the slot machines at Caesars. What else!

"I had a sore shoulder," she recalls. "I wanted to stop playing. . .I was down to my last three coins. That's when I hit the triple bars." The payoff was $1,150,697, not a bad wedding gift. The couple had been living with her parents, saving money as they prepared for married life. "More than likely, we'll buy a house," Lorraine says now. Added her new husband, "And I want to get her a nicer wedding ring."

Of course, the neat refrain of sweet Lorraine loses something when it becomes "The Case Of The Goofy Grease Monkey." An auto mechanic hit a $250,000 slot machine jackpot at the Las Vegas Hilton. That should be the end of that, except he came back to the same resort almost two years later to the day and won $2.1 million *more* on another slot machine. "I feel like a hero," he said. "I'm going to retire and come here every weekend." This is good news for Las Vegas. . .bad news for the player. He dribbled away the first quarter of a million in less than a year — on the slot machines at the Hilton!

Evelyn Marie Adams won $1.5 million in a New Jersey lottery in 1986, about a year after collecting $3.9 million in another New Jersey state lottery. "It was such a shock," she said. "To think, I've got so much money, and now to know I've got more." Yeah, yeah sure, Evelyn. The odds of her winning two lotteries like that were only one in approximately 15 trillion.

The amount of money won by these individuals almost numbs the senses. . . one million, three-point-nine million, nearly five million. The zeros seem to go on forever, and it makes a person wonder what it feels like to be on the receiving end of such a windfall, or if there is any such thing as bad luck posing as good.

An Arkansas family came to Las Vegas, heading

straight for the "Million Dollar Baby" slot arcade at Caesars Palace. One member of the family struck it rich, becoming a "million dollar baby" himself. Unfortunately, he *was* a baby. . .at least in the eyes of the Nevada Gaming Control Board. The player was only 19 years old (Nevada law prohibits anyone under the age of 21 from gambling) and therefore he was not entitled to the $1,061,811 he won.

For a brief moment the young lad had shaken off his earthly shrouds and danced with the gods, but it turned out to be the "Minute Waltz." In the National Enquirer, he told what it was like:

"It all started with a simple blip-blip-blip as three bars lined up on the slot machine screen, and I was a winner. 'I'm a millionaire,' I thought. 'I'll never have to work again. I'm rich.' A speedboat raced across my mind. Then came a car — a red Corvette convertible. 'I can't believe it,' I said. 'I'm only nineteen — and I have it made.' Or so I thought."

Caesars was willing to pay the jackpot, but the Gaming Control Board said no. State officials explained that the hotel could lose its gaming license if the minor were paid.

It would be a frustrating experience for anybody knowing that every day for the rest of one's life the same mad line would click through the mind, "I had a million $, I had a million $, I had a million $. . ." That red Corvette may be his someday, but he will make payments on it like everyone else — just because his body was not on this planet two years sooner.

True gamblers scoff at slot machines and state lotteries

and anything else that is more chance than circumstance. According to a lottery spokesperson, it is "because they can't control the randomness of winning." Anyone can pull a slot machine handle and win a few thousand, or throw the dice for half an hour. That is luck, pure and simple. A real gambler likes something he can sink his teeth into, like good old-fashioned football.

John Malone is a blackjack floorman at the Dunes in Las Vegas. One November he won the sum of $100,000 from the Barbary Coast by parlaying a lowly $5 bill in two frenzied days of football. To do this, he had to correctly forecast the results of 15 straight college and professional football games, and he had to cover the spread in every single one. It was a 160,000 to 1 longshot and had never been done before.

Malone won his bet, otherwise the story would not be important. What is more significant, however, is his state of mind at the time he won and how he felt when he realized all that money was his. "I just sat down for 20 minutes," he told this writer. "I didn't quite know what to think. The biggest thing that went through my mind, after I won, was 'Did I circle my ticket right?' And then I thought, 'Why me? Why was I the guy that did it?' But you know, I'm a firm believer that everybody is going to have one given day in their life when they're going to get lucky. I sweated seven years to get mine."

Some of the things that happen every day of the year in Nevada casinos might fare well as plots for television shows, but who would believe them? For instance, a woman went into a casino at Stateline, began playing a $5 slot machine, and eventually won jackpots totaling $4,200. Out of her winnings she bought a special $100 token to try her luck at a brand new hundred dollar slot machine that had just been installed. Georgia Simpson pulled the handle, and out cascaded ten thousand dollars. There's a signpost up ahead; Georgia has just crossed over into — The Twilight Zone.

In California, a housewife won $6.7 million in the state Lotto game, and described her feelings thusly: "I almost had a heart attack." She learned of her good fortune while watching the Lotto drawing on television, was unable to sleep that night, and the next morning her husband told his boss to take a hike.

That is what people want to hear. They do not want to listen to some lucky jerk blow off about continuing his present life style while his winnings are being compounded semi-annually. That is boring. A real American would quit his job (naturally), his wife would take a month off work, they would dump their house and move into a condo on the beach, and they would buy everything on the face of the earth. Then, in a year's time, the guy would be broke and working again, just like everybody else.

You see it in the newspapers every week or so. A name without a face wins a lottery somewhere, and there is a short blurb about it buried under the weather map. People never read these things since they are like little fairy tales that only happen to other people who do not even need the money in the first place, and besides they can't be sitting around the house scrutinizing the newspaper all day because they have to go to work and make some money!

Behind every glowing winner, at whatever game of chance, stand hundreds upon hundreds of weary and worn losers. The camera never shows them, but they are the ones who created the winner in the first place, shooting the odds and the payoffs up to the moon and back. We do not know their names, for no photographer takes their picture. No parables appear in the press.

Gamblers Anonymous figures there are somewhere between three and six million compulsive gamblers out there — 400,000 in New Jersey alone — so in all actuality this estimate is probably on the low side. The stories one hears from this institution and others like it represent tragedy at its zenith, life on the off ramp. . .the bittersweet tailspins of human lives out of control.

"My name is Harold," a tale will begin, and the rest of it is always the same: "I am a compulsive gambler." Harold got his first taste of gambling at the age of eleven, when he stumbled onto a teenage group of boys shooting craps, winding up $3.25 to the good. "Why do I have to work so hard to make money delivering newspapers when I can gamble and get it that much quicker, and easier?" he thought to himself. "I think that was the first time my mind ever worked that way."

Two years later he got into a tic-tac-toe game with an older (and wiser) youth, who beat him out of a penny and then let Harold go double or nothing. The amount went from one cent to two, then four, and so on until Harold owed the larger boy the staggering sum of $325, which he paid by selling his coin collection.

"By the time I was 13, I was betting horses through a bookie. I used to put my notebook up on my desk and pretend that I was doing my homework. Actually, I had a racing form inside and I was handicapping the horses for that day. Then, at recess, I would use the pay phone at school to call the book and place my bets. I also went to the track whenever I could. Children accompanied by parents got in the track free, and I would talk some stranger into walking me through the gate as his child.

"Between the ages of 15 and 19 I did most of my gambling on arcade machines. One time I lost $200 to another boy on a tennis ball machine. It was a machine where you hit a padded handle to knock the tennis ball up to the top, and it would drop down into numbered rings. I was betting on the high score. It was a stupid game but I liked the action. At that time, I was making $140 a week selling magazine subscriptions."

Later Harold discovered Jai Alai in Tijuana, and for funds once sold a broken wristwatch which he set to the correct time, telling the Mexican jeweler that the watch was so expensive you couldn't hear it tick. You have to give Harold "e" for "efforta." He got two bucks for it, which was enough for a full bet on the next Jai Alai game.

The sordid story went on and on, and even Clint Eastwood would have wiped away a tear. Harold got hooked on cards, got hooked himself, got divorced, got hooked on basketball, got bailed out of a jam by his mom (who had to cash in her life insurance policy), got to Las Vegas, got a job, got married again, got busted again, and finally got religion. In this case it was Gamblers Anonymous, about which Harold says now, "If you feel you're not bad enough to join, then you're eligible too."

When you listen to Harold talk, and you watch the firm line of his mouth and the misty bloom in his eyes, you feel a sort of proud sympathy for him. He shucked everything but a sliver of self-respect, and he is crawling to his feet very slowly. "We lose three things to gambling," he said. "Time, money and a sense of values."

Rod tells the next story. "It's Sunday, three a.m. I'm sitting in my car on the top floor of a parking garage in stunned silence, at the realization of where my actions of the past few hours have taken me. I am a compulsive gambler, and in my relentless quest to satisfy my disease, have once again been unable to live up to the promises made to my family."

"Saturday was a pretty routine day at the office, so I called home to let my wife know I'd be home in a little while, hung up the phone and headed for my favorite casino."

PAYCHECKS CASHED HERE.

"I only had twenty dollars with me, but in my mind it would be enough to make the score I was looking for."

The time is 6:15.

"I bought two rolls of quarters, selected a slot machine and began to play."

The time is 6:35.

"I was broke and angry. My plan failed, as it always did before. I had to at least get that twenty back, but how? I'm broke, but I can't be a loser again."

Rod got a brainstorm. The safe in the office!

"No thought of stopping now. My disease tells me I'm in big trouble and have to get even. It drives me on and on, to sink deeper into the hole I am creating. Now the safe is empty..." Oh no!!

"...and now I sit in my car. Replacing the money is impossible, and in a few hours everyone will know what I've done. Should I run? Start the car? I could put it in drive, go over the edge, and in ten seconds it will all be over. But what if I live? The only thing to do is...face the music."

Rod faced the music, even wrote the words, and his song is called "The Last Bet," thanks to Gamblers Anonymous. There are other organizations that help, including the National Council on Compulsive Gambling. Howard

Cornbleth is on that council's board of directors and is also a gambling counselor at Charter Hospital in Las Vegas. In his words, "I judge a compulsive gambler by what his thoughts are. The amount of the bet is not important, but the gambler's frame of mind is."

In his booklet *Profile Of Pathological Gamblers*, Dr. Robert Custer states that a compulsive gambler goes through phases. First is the winning phase, then the losing phase, and finally the desperation phase. Custer says that a compulsive gambler will usually ignore his symptoms until reaching this last phase, because losing is intolerable and he must get his money back. The gambler will begin to miss work, then see less and less of his family which in turn causes a deterioration of his home life.

It is no wonder then that the rate of attempted suicides by this type of gambler is 160 times the national average, according to Cornbleth. He added that 20 to 25 percent of compulsive gamblers have attempted to take their own lives.

There was a man from Texas who did something terrible on his first trip to Las Vegas. He won $70,000 shooting craps. After that he went downhill faster than a burned out oil well, winding up not only a compulsive gambler but one with overpowering suicidal tendencies to boot.

He walked to the Union Plaza in downtown Vegas, and headed up the stairs to the top of the building. A locked door on the fifth floor stopped him from going any higher, so he went down the street to the Golden Nugget. Getting to the roof, he started for the edge and his rendezvous with Saint Peter. A worker stopped him. "Sorry buddy, this is a construction area." The gambler thought fast (average IQ of compulsive gambler is 120) and countered, "I'm an inspector, with — uh — Acme Construction Company."

"If you're an inspector you got to wear a hard hat."

The gambler stopped in his tracks. Here he was getting ready to kill himself, and he was walking around on top of the Golden Nugget with a goddamn helmet on! If he went to his death like this, he would be the laughing stock of Cameron County!

That is when he looked in the yellow pages and called Charter Hospital for help.

Another story, one without a happy ending, concerns the man who made headlines when he won $750,000 on a single bet at the Horseshoe in Las Vegas. Four years later he lost a cool million on one bet at the same casino, and then killed himself with an overdose of drugs. He left a suicide note and instructions that the following plaque be placed on the urn containing his ashes: "The Phantom Gambler At The Horseshoe Who Lost A Million Dollars."

There was a lady who got so mesmerized with her state's lottery that she would spend all her cash on lottery tickets, including most of the money from her grocery budget. She began to feed her husband tasty little casseroles made out of stuff like dog food. The guy was a good sport about it, though. When he found out he said, "The funny thing is, it really doesn't taste bad if you fix it right. I sort of got used to it. My favorite was her mystery meatloaf." Pass the catsup, please.

A retired Air Force officer moved to Las Vegas where he soon became a compulsive gambler. He received a monthly pension check for $1,600, but he would be broke in a week's time. The rest of the month would be spent eating free breakfasts with fun book coupons, looking for stray coins on the sidewalk, and sleeping in a local graveyard because the parks were too crowded with other compulsive gamblers.

Nicholas Dandalos was reputed to be a compulsive gambler. We know him better as the legendary Nick the Greek. "He was my idol at one time," said a member of Gamblers Anonymous. "When he died he was 84 years old. He had never done anything but gamble his whole life. He was four million dollars in debt, and there was no money for even a funeral. He was buried in a pauper's grave in North Las Vegas."

We shot this question at Howard Cornbleth, the peer counselor for the compulsive gambling treatment program at Charter Hospital. "Is it possible for someone to become a compulsive gambler just by playing slot machines?"

"Absolutely. In fact, the biggest thing I've seen today are the people who play video poker machines. Ninety percent of compulsive gamblers in the Las Vegas area are hooked on them."

A man and a woman were seated next to each other at a meeting of Gamblers Anonymous a year or so back. The woman had stolen money from her children to play video poker, and comtemplated suicide after losing several hundred dollars. The man lost $70,000 on a poker machine that took 20 five-dollar tokens at a time. He would lose more in two minutes than the woman had lost altogether. She beat her habit, quite possibly because her kids started hiding their piggy banks, but the man lost his wife and his business and at last report never did overcome his addiction.

There is no exact profile of a compulsive gambler. Cornbleth says it can be a person from seven to 70. "But in most cases, it is generally a man in his thirties who starts writing hot checks or steals. . . not because he is a thief but because he is in trouble with banks, shylocks, finance companies. He thinks he will get out of this mess, but he can't." He has no social life, no friends. He is tense and irritable, sleeps poorly, eats irregularly and drinks alcohol more. Cornbleth went on to say, "If he is betting something that he can afford, it is no fun. He has to bet more, in order to make it exciting."

Even the occasional winner will sometimes find fame and fortune not entirely to his liking. William Walker of Strasburg, Illinois, won $1 million in that state's lottery. Walker, a truck driver, told what it was like in an interview with one of the TV networks.

"I would say it is a devoted headache. . . People think that I won a million dollars and they don't sit back and think that that's divided over a 20-year period." Walker gets $38,250 a year in twenty-one installments.

"After I got my first check, I got out of debt and I was out of debt for 15 minutes. I went right on through her just like I knowed what I was doing. I mean, I had worked all my life hard and never did have a new car or a new pickup or anything like that, and when I won it I went out and bought 'em."

Walker got a new car, took his family to Hawaii, moved to a bigger house across the street and spent $30,000 remodeling it. His health started to deteriorate. "I can truthfully say I was never sick a day in my life, till after I won that money. I got to the point where I couldn't cope with people. I mean, I was hiding from them." He spent five years learning to manage his money; he does not trust anyone now because they took advantage of him before.

"It's to the point now that instead of being in a crowd, you just as soon be off someplace with one or two persons or by yourself. But there ain't no doubt in my mind that I'm gonna win that lottery again. I'm gonna *have* to win again to take care of this first one. I mean, I've gotten so

much trouble over this first million that I'm gonna have
to win another million so I can have a good time.''

CHAPTER 4

Hot Tables!

I never saw the dice, but the man who told me the story said they were like any other pair: clear red plastic, with bold little white dots that you could read from a hundred yards. The corners were still sharp enough to draw blood, and the name "Harrah's Tahoe" was as clean on both as the day they were used: March 18, 1961.

A cold wind was coming off Lake Tahoe, and most of the tables were busy at Harrah's on the south shore. The bartender grimaced as another customer ordered a Margarita, but his words were lost when a roar went up from the nearby dice table.

The nondescript man holding the dice had rolled his third straight 7, and his partner was leading the cheers. The partner knew just enough about the game to drive the dealers crazy.

Another roar from the crowd. The man with the dice, later to be known as "the miracle shooter," had rolled his fourth 7. A player at the other end of the table shook his head, and plunked another dollar on the "Don't Pass."

The dice whirled through the air once more. "Winner seven," the stickman said, and the crowd roared again.

Another roll, another 7. The noise by now was deafening, and onlookers strained to see this mystery man. "Damnedest thing," one of them said to a woman behind him. "He just rolled his seventh straight 7."

By now the "don't" player was busted. He backed away, and his place was immediately swallowed by another player. Bills landed on the table, and bets were placed in almost pleading voices. The miracle shooter rolled a 5, and then a winner 5. The miracle shooter rolled a 9, and then a winner 9. Six. Winner 6. Winner 7. Eight. Winner 8. Eleven.

"The amateurs had dreamed of such rolls as this," wrote New York Mirror reporter Bill Slocum. "The pros just knew it couldn't be done, and they were watching it being done...their faces wrinkled in disbelief with each successive roll. Then the miracle man turned human. He rolled a 5, then a 7. It was all over." The hottest roll in the history of Nevada had ended.

The shooter and his partner won $3800. Another man, who came to the table with $12, left with $4200. Three other players won $500 each. The 32-pass hand lasted for 37 minutes.

Sands executive host Vic Vickrey is based in Dallas, but flies to Las Vegas several times a month. In fact, he has flown on the same plane so many times that he is always recognized by the flight attendants. On one of his most recent flights, the stewardess asked him, "How can you fly to Las Vegas so often? You must be a good gambler." Vickrey laughed. "You're right, honey. I never lose." Before the plane landed, word had circulated that Lady

Luck's bosom buddy was sitting in seat 16A. "I met the pilot, the co-pilot, and everybody else. The only thing I was wondering about was who was flying the damn airplane!"

Everybody loves a winner. Watch a shooter at the dice table who makes a few passes. Suddenly he is everybody's friend. Then watch what happens when the inevitable "loser seven" rears its ugly head. "Ahhh, you didn't hit the end, you stupid idiot." For a tiny flick of an instant, though, he was *somebody*.

A woman, appearing to be in her mid-thirties, put two dollars on the pass line at a Las Vegas craps table. "What do I do now?" she asked the dealers. "Pick up two dice and throw them to the other end," the stickman coached her.

An hour and a half elapsed before she finally relinquished those two dice. It was the stuff of dreams — the big hand, the hot table, the streak a gambler spends his waking hours trying to find and ride to glory.

The woman won something like $80, but the other players — most of whom were die-hard regulars in the Strip casino — took the place for $600,000. Hoisting the woman on their shoulders, the players carried her around the table whooping and hollering like she had just scored the winning touchdown in the Rose Bowl.

Watching all this take place was the casino manager. He approached the woman at the cashier's cage, where she was busy counting the chips the other players had given her. He would get her name and other pertinent data from her driver's license, and issue a national press release about her amazing run of luck.

Then he spotted her date of birth on the license, and his blood went cold. The woman was only twenty years old!

If the gaming control board found out about this, the casino could lose its license or face a stiff fine. Needless to say, this was one story that never made the papers. The woman was escorted to the front door — and anonymity — by security guards.

Yet she had done something that every gambler would kill for. She stopped time for one mythical magical moment and saw everything fall neatly into place. Ask an old veteran about this, someone who has stood behind the tables for a few dreary decades, and he will nod his head knowingly. "Sure, you're going to have times when the dice get out of line, or a deck of cards goes bad. I remember once when this guy hit us for $240,000. It was on the craps table, and he couldn't lose. He'd bet on the line. Winner seven. He'd bet in the field. Twelve craps. He'd bet on the big six. Six easy. He'd bet against the dice. Loser seven. But something like that, it happens only once in ten lifetimes."

Horseshoe casino manager Tony Cook says, "There was a craps dealer at the Riviera a few years ago that got on a roll. He started out with spit — two or three hundred — and won close to a million dollars over a period of about six weeks. He was playing dice; he was playing everything. Lady Luck was shining on him, and he won a lot of money. He just got on a run."

On a recent New Year's Eve, a player sat down at a Horseshoe blackjack table. Before the smoke cleared two hours later, he had pocketed nearly two million dollars! "He won his first bet,' Cook recalled, "and never looked back. He was betting anywhere from $5,000 to $25,000 a hand, and he just got a good run going. But when you think about it, it's not that big in numbers, not when you look at the relativity of it all. If he's betting $25,000, he only had to win 40 more bets than he lost to win a million dollars. It's the same principle as a guy starting with $25 and winning a thousand." That makes the rest of us feel a little better when we start with $25 and lose a thousand. Just think, we could have lost a *million*.

In the early 1950s, a casino partnership was dissolved because of a hot streak. In this instance, it was a hot streak for the house — not the player. A Texan lost $250,000 in a downtown Las Vegas casino, most of which had been extended to the player on credit. The Texan promised to send the money, but one of the partners was less than optimistic that the money would ever be received. "This is no good," he said to the other partner, who had given the gambler the credit. "The guy's not going to pay." "Yes, he is," the partner said. The standoff was settled by one partner taking the casino, and the other taking the $250,000 marker. By the way, the Texan paid the marker, and the ousted partner used the money to open another casino across the street.

More recently, a Houston oilman came to Las Vegas with $300,000 in cash, and after a grueling eight-hour stint at the dice table he was down to his last $1,500. He threw the chips to the stickman. "Eleven this roll," he said wearily. Up came the pit boss. "Sorry, Mister D. That's over the limit, we can't book it." After a brief discussion, the oilman changed his bet to $500 on eleven and the other thousand on seven. Boom, *winner seven,* and a payoff of $4,000! When the hand ended, the Texas gambler had won back his $300,000, while the pit boss was telling both his friends, "This guy turned a toothpick into a lumber yard!"

The biggest dice hand in history did not occur in Las Vegas. . .or Atlantic City. . .or Monte Carlo. It happened in Miami, Florida, in 1946. A woman, at the urging of her husband, picked up the dice at a private club. One hour passed. The club was down $250,000. Another hour churned by. The club was down half a million. Fifteen more minutes went past, and that was it. No, she did not crap out. The club did. With its bankroll gone, and its secondary bankroll depleted, the owner closed the table. From this historic incident came the expression: "Unfinished Hand." Believe it — or not.

At the Dunes Hotel in Las Vegas, a woman (why is it always a woman?) held the dice for two hours, from 2 o'clock on a sleepy Sunday afternoon until 4 p.m. It happened while a New York junket was in the hotel, and the table lost $300,000. The hotel gained ten times that much in publicity, however, as the next day the story even made the Paul Harvey newscast. There is a funny footnote to this story. After the hand ended, one of the hotel's owners was being consoled by the pit boss. "Think of all the great publicity this will bring the hotel," the pit boss said to him. The owner growled, "Hell, that's what we've got *matchbooks* for!"

The gods of chance must nod off from time to time, however, as there are many examples of strange behavior by dice and cards and roulette balls. These objects do things that defy all rules of logic and mathematics, much to the dismay of bosses and casino owners. As a matter of fact, one-time Dunes owner Major Riddle is said to have had a dice table hauled to the back parking lot after a losing day, where he personally chopped it to pieces with a fire ax. "Take that, you blankety blank," he was heard to say, as wood chips rained down from the sky.

There was a row of slot machines positioned next to the showroom in another Vegas casino. Whenever a jackpot was hit on one of the machines, the hotel owner would have it disconnected. Eventually the day came when every single machine in sight was "out of order." The hotel owner was also known to change stickmen at the dice table should a player win anything. On one occasion, a dealer came into the casino on his day off to pick up his paycheck. He had been painting his house, and was wearing a pair of paint-splattered overalls. The hotel owner spotted him. "Go in on the stick," he said, "and whack that guy out." The dealer's first call was, "Winner six the hard way." He was immediately taken off the game and sent back home.

It seems that no section of the casino is safe when mathematical probability takes a holiday. A young man walked up to a Las Vegas blackjack table with two $5 chips and won 23 straight hands. Dealer Ginny Cooper said the man's highest bet was $400, and he left the casino with $3700. In another incident, a player got eight blackjacks out of nine hands, while at the Stardust a craps shooter once rolled 36 consecutive passes. Unfortunately, he was betting *against* the dice at the time.

Another long hand ended abruptly when the shooter suffered a heart attack just as he let go of the dice. The first thing he said when he regained consciousness was, "Did I make my point?"

Playing keno at a downtown Vegas club, a man spent 50 cents on an 8-spot ticket. Lo and behold, all eight numbers came up in the following game for a payoff of $12,500. True to form, casino guards surrounded the man while an investigation ensued. Meanwhile, the man played the same numbers in the next game, and here came those same eight numbers! By this time the first $12,500 was in his pocket, but the security guards again had the man in custody. It was too much for the "lucky" winner. While his second ticket was being checked, he dropped dead of a heart attack.

Another man hit a keno ticket for $1600. Elation turned to outrage, however, when he was informed he would have to pay taxes on his winnings. He had just lost $30,000 at the baccarat tables!

A local gambler went to the Riviera Hotel with $300. Hearing screams of excitement at one of the dice tables, the gambler shouldered his way through the crowd. "Give me all the numbers," he said to the dealer. By the time the hand was over, the man had won $4200. He went to the Sands Hotel, where he spotted a crowd at another dice table. Again, he shoved his way through the people, only to realize that this crowd had gathered because Frank Sinatra was throwing the dice. The gambler could not resist. "Give me all the numbers," he cried. Sinatra did not shoot a newsworthy hand, but several others did. Four hours later the gambler walked away with $15,000. Unable to sleep, he continued to patrol the Las Vegas Strip like a junkie looking for a fix. In five days time he accumulated $87,000, and now he was living in a suite at the Riviera, where his run of luck began.

Then he lost $3,000 at blackjack. Another $8,000 went through his fingers at the craps table. Should he stop? Should he keep playing, and try to win it back? "Give me all the numbers," he said on an impulse. "Seven loser," the stickman called, and now he was down another $3,200. There wasn't much for the gambler to pack when he left the Riviera two days later. Just a couple of shirts, and a toothbrush, and five $10 bills. It was all that was left of the gambler's $87,000.

A casino executive was once treated to a gourmet meal by a friend working in another resort. After dinner, the man stopped at one of the hotel's blackjack tables. All he really wanted to do was pay for his meal by gambling a little, and under the circumstances $40 seemed about right. He never lost a hand, and walked away with nearly $15,000. The man went to another casino, where his incredible run of luck continued. By now he had nearly $40,000! The next day he bought himself a brand new car, and decided to press his luck at the tables with the rest of his winnings. Before the night was over, he had lost all the money and wrecked the car on his way home.

Yes, behind every silver lining lurks a big black cloud. Take the man who walked up to a dice table with $50. Two hours later — by perseverance and luck — he had accumulated $1,200. Too tired to stand any longer, he found a seat at a $100 blackjack game. As he sat down, he gave himself a mental command. He would stop gambling as soon as he reached $5,000. He lost twelve hands in a row. "I never even got to see the dealer shuffle," he remembered sadly.

An army corporal shot his way into the record books at a Golden Nugget craps table. And it might never have happened at all, if not for a Texan wearing a Stetson hat. When the soldier first picked up the dice, he threw a nine for a point. On his next throw, one of the dice landed on the brim of the hat, then bounced back onto the table. It was a winner nine, and the start of a one hour and 45 minute hand.

A woman began playing roulette in a Vegas casino with $400. She was betting $50 at a time on 4-number combinations, or what is known in gambling circles as "corner bets." Six hours later, she walked away with $200,000. Casino personnel were so suspicious they dismantled the wheel and had it examined. Finding nothing wrong, they told the roulette supervisor that the woman must have used "some type of electrical device." "Oh?" said the supervisor. "And what kind of electrical device did she use?" He never got an answer. Incidentally, the numbers played by the woman were 1, 2, 4 and 5; 8, 9, 11 and 12.

A wheel dealer recalls when black came up 20 straight times at the roulette table. The most instances of the ball landing in the same slot was five times in a row, and the number was 17. "I know," said the dealer who was there, "because somebody was betting five dollars on it for me." That, by the way, is the most popular number on the roulette wheel, chiefly because 17 is the one James Bond always bets on in the movies. It is also the center number on the roulette layout.

Nine straight 7's came up on a Vegas dice table, and there is documentation of seven consecutive 11's being rolled. Four 12's were rolled in succession at the Las Vegas Hilton, one witness to that feat being none other than Colonel Tom Parker, Elvis Presley's manager. He bet $700 on 12 after the third one rolled, and took down a payoff of $21,000. Granted, that's not much money for a man of Colonel Parker's stature, but "that's all right, mama." It beats being "down in the ghetto." Parker must have been wearing his "good luck charm."

At the Stardust, a player bet $20 on 12 at the craps table. The 12 rolled. The player bet $40 on 12. The 12 rolled. The player got permission to bet $500 on 12. The 12 rolled. The player walked away with over $17,000, defying mathematical odds of 42,874 to 1. At the Mint Casino, a player asked to bet $200 on 12, which the floorman let him do. The 12 rolled, and the player got $6,200. It was not an extremely large amount of money, but enough to get the pit boss to the table in a hurry. "How could you let somebody bet that much money on 12?'' the pit boss demanded. The floor-man scratched his head. "I didn't think he could make it," he finally answered.

Donn Knepp, in his book *Las Vegas, The Entertainment Capital*, tells of a gambler who rolled 28 straight passes at the dice table, only to walk away with a paltry $750. "Little did he realize that such an occurrence was a million to one happening," Knepp wrote, "and one that could have netted him enough money to buy the state of Nevada. Had he parlayed every single bet, he would have won $289,406,976.'' The house limits would have prevented this, of course, but it does make for a good story.

At the Desert Inn, a player at the dice table made his point of 10 three times in a row, and made it the hard way (two 5's) each time! Are you with us on this one? The player rolled a ten, rolled it again the hard way to make his point, rolled 10 again on the come-out, then rolled it the hard way again to make his point; he rolled 10 a fifth time, and then rolled it again, the hard way, to make his point. To figure the odds on such a thing happening, I put a pencil to it and here are my compilations:

To establish a point of 10, the odds are 11 to 1. Of the 36 ways the dice can come up, 3 ways are a 10 (6-4, 4-6 and 5-5). That leaves 33 ways for some other number. There-fore, the odds are 33 to 3, reduced to 11 to 1. Now, the odds to make the point the hard way (two fives) are 8 to 1, since there are 8 ways to miss — the six ways of rolling a 7 and the two ways of rolling an 'easy' 10 (6-4, 4-6). So we simply multiply both numbers to determine the odds of establishing a point of 10 and making it the hard way: 8 × 11 = 88. The odds are 87 to 1. To do it *three* times in a row, we multiply the odds three times: 88 × 88 × 88 minus 1 to 1. Or: 681,471 to 1. In other words, it ain't "easy!"

Of course, by the time anyone worked out these equations, the shooter had checked out of the Desert Inn ...went back to California...got married...had three children...bought a book called "How To Retire On Your I.R.A."...quit his job...and moved into a bomb shelter on the island of Kauai in the South Pacific.

A player walked up to a dice table at the Sahara with two $5 chips. He lost the first one when he rolled a craps, but parlayed his other $5 chip to $10, then $20, $40, $80, and right on up...eventually cashing out $1,600. Boxman Jim Sinay, who was supervising the game, told the dice crew, "We will never see that happen again." Just then the player returned to the game — with a $5 chip — which he snowballed into another $1,200!

At exactly 3:15 one afternoon, a man picked up the dice in a Las Vegas casino. He told his friend, "Stan, you might have to loan me some money. I've only got $25 left." Well, he never had to borrow any money from Stan. When the hand ended exactly one hour later, the man walked away with $80,000. That, however, is not the end of the story. The following day, at exactly 3:15 in the afternoon, another player came up to the same table and he too shot the dice for exactly one hour. The only difference was that the second player only won $40,000. The next afternoon at 3:15, the table was closed, but it was opened again, one hour later.

It would seem that casino owners had the foresight and wisdom to seize advantage of situations like these. In 1951, the Desert Inn encased two dice in a silver frame nestled on a velvet pillow. A bronze plaque tersely told the story: "THESE DICE MADE 28 CONSECUTIVE PASSES." The dice vanished, however, as did a similar pair at the Sahara, where a woman threw 28 passes in 1982. She wound up with $55 while the casino blew an estimated $800,000. The dice went on public display, but they were eventually replaced by a boring old golf trophy.

Certainly it would stir men's souls to behold such instruments of fate, but these articles are apparently looked upon now as ungrateful traitors that do not belong in the same house with good little dice and cards. Maybe the dice were sold to somebody. Maybe they were taken out of the casino in the dead of night and buried in the desert. Maybe they were just filed away in an old cardboard box somewhere, where they sit forgotten to this day.

The trouble with today's casino operators is that they have no feeling for history. When the Desert Inn opened in 1950, the casino's roulette wheel was the center of attention. Complete with little scenes of Nevada folklore, the hand-carved wheel was personally designed by owner Wilbur Clark. For nearly 40 years the wheel spun its way through good times and bad. Then the casino changed hands. One of the first moves by the new owners was to get rid of the old roulette wheel, which did not fit in with the Desert Inn's glassy new image. This marvelous relic of a time gone by was sold to a gaming equipment salesman for $250! Why, the casino could have made 50 times that much, selling admissions to see it. Instead, this bit of history is just an entry on a ledger form. New Roulette Wheel: $4800 (Less Trade) $4550. Yawn.

Rumors abound of a blackjack table being covered with black cloth after a losing day, or of a dice table closed during a hot hand. Perhaps these things have happened, almost assuredly they did during the wild early years in Las Vegas, when even dealers were run out the door for conspiring to be a party to such dastardly circumstance.

One shift boss, who was an avid gambler himself, had

his own way of dealing with matters when the casino's luck took a wrong turn. He would retreat to the hotel kitchen and fry fish until things got back to normal. On other occasions the shift boss, who stood only five feet tall, would dress up in women's clothing and flirt with the dealers, hoping that this would "break their concentration." Another time a player at the dice table lost his false teeth just as he leaned over to make a bet. The shift boss popped out his own fake dentures, and shoved them across the table. "You're faded!" he cried.*

Many years ago, a casino owner became known around town for his temper tantrums, especially when the fickle finger of fate gave him the high sign. He would change the house limit at the craps table right in the middle of a big hand, dropping the maximum bet from $4,000 down to $500. If this did not smolder enthusiasm, he would call "no roll" when the dice were not thrown to the end of the table, except in the instance of a loser seven. Then it was okay.

"The man was a cool customer," laughed a former employee. "He lived right in the hotel, and if the house was losing money he would come downstairs in his bathrobe. I saw him go up to a craps table during a big hand and stop the game to look at the dice. He turned them over in his hand for five minutes, inspecting the corners and checking the spots. Then he tossed the dice back on the table and walked away. The only thing was, he threw a different pair of dice back. He still had the other ones in his hand."

This same hotel owner once found himself being introduced to a woman gambler who had just checked into his hotel with $50,000. He saw that she was given the red

---

*"Faded" is a gambling term meaning that the house has covered, or accepted, your bet.

carpet treatment, with dinner in the gourmet restaurant and a front booth for the midnight show. Then he invited her to his office, where he told her it was silly for her to be gambling with $50,000 — which she would probably lose — and instead she should invest it in his hotel — which she did. A week later he declared bankruptcy, and the woman wound up losing her money anyway.

Then there was the casino manager in another popular Las Vegas hotel, whose reputation as a skinflint practically eclipsed that of Scrooge himself. A down-and-out gambler once had the 39-cent breakfast in the hotel's coffee shop, and then found himself without the necessary funds to settle his bill. The casino manager had the man charged with "defrauding an innkeeper," and he was taken out of the restaurant in handcuffs.

"I was working in the baccarat pit at Caesars Palace," Tony Cook remembers, "and we had some high-playing Orientals in. The president of the hotel came by on his way to breakfast, leaned over the rail and said, 'Tony, how are you doing?' I went over and said, 'We're doing real good right now; we're winning 1.2 million.' 'Oh, wonderful, wonderful.' He went to breakfast, and came back in about 30 minutes. 'How are we doing now?' I said, 'Well, right now we're stuck about $800,000.' He said, 'Jesus Christ, how can you be stuck $800,000? You were just winning 1.2 million!' I said, 'Well, we're gambling here; we're not selling bread!' "

There will always be that invisible rift between corporate casino people and those who came up through the ranks. An ex-owner of the Aladdin reluctantly took a job as executive host at the Tropicana. While having lunch with the hotel president one day, a high roller stopped at the table to say hello. The host invited the gambler to join them, and afterwards the hotel president signed for the meal with a flourish of his pen. "Let me get the tip," the gambler said, but the hotel president shook his head. Both quietly watched as the president withdrew a small plastic coin holder, and slowly counted out seven quarters and a dime. This was too much for the high roller, who threw a $20 bill on the table and stormed off. "I'll never play in this lousy place again," he called over his shoulder. The host quit his job the next day.

Later it was rumored that the former Aladdin owner was taking night classes at a local college. A reporter called him to verify the story. "That's right," he said. "I'm majoring in accounting, so I can get me a blankety blank job in one of these blankety blank casinos!"

When all is said and done, it really comes down to one thing. There will always be hot streaks at the dice tables, hot cards at the blackjack tables, hot slots up and down trash-strewn passageways. The casinos cannot win all the money, or gambling would simply disappear. Yet at the same time, it never hurts to give the losers something too.

This is what Las Vegas has lost. No one kisses the losers anymore. There was a time when a man could gamble freely, knowing that if he lost his money there was somebody in charge who would give him a bus ticket home. At the very least, he was assured of something to eat. It was one of those little-known facts of life that was passed quietly from generation to generation. By the time a man gets a free meal nowadays, he barely has enough strength to pick the parsley out of his potato salad.

After all, how much does it really cost to "comp" gamblers to a plate of food — not just high rollers but anyone who has stood at a dice table for half an afternoon? How much does it cost to give playing cards or used dice to anyone who wants them? How much does it cost to comp an otherwise empty seat in the showroom? How much does it cost to drive somebody to the airport, when he has been gambling for three solid days?

The answer from the corporations is always the same. "We do not have the resources to allocate the necessary capital so that each of our businesses is able to compete as effectively as possible." That, by the way, is a direct quote from someone who makes about $250,000 a year.

It almost makes one reach for the Kleenex box, until you read where the Hilton Corporation spent $100 million recently just to touch up the Las Vegas Hilton and the Flamingo. What we want to know is where Hilton got all that money in the first place.

Maybe it is time Las Vegas got back to basics. A successful casino operator does not need a Ph.D. from M.I.T. He just needs to know something about people. Marie Antoinette lost the crown (and what the crown was sitting upon) when she said, "Let them eat cake." If only she had said, "Let them eat *free* cake," she would have been the toast of Paris.

Meanwhile, if you happen to see a weary man trudging alone through a noisy casino, his eyes furtively searching every nook and darkened wall, say hello. It is just me, still looking for that pair of dice in a silver frame. Sitting on a velvet pillow.

CHAPTER 5

Tools Of The Trade

Gambling has gone from the back rooms of shanty town to respectability on Wall Street, all in the course of a hundred years. It was easy to set up shop in the beginning. All that was needed were a couple of dice, a deck of cards, a few painted women, a bottle of red eye, and some unsuspecting suckers who poured into the gaming tents in droves.

One of the oldest theories as to the origin of playing cards was that they were brought from India by wandering gypsies who used them to tell fortunes...usually something like, "You are about to be shafted out of every sheckle in your satchel. Oh, and you'll live to a ripe old age and have many grandchildren." The cards were much diffcrent from the Bicycle playing cards of today, round discs of thin wood and ivory either painted or lacquered.

Years passed, and although gambling never really changed, the equipment did. Punch boards were popular for awhile, with a customer investing his pocket change trying to win anything from twenty cigarettes up to a super colossal grand prize of 64 dollars. Unfortunately, they were being sold mostly by grown-ups to mostly school kids who won mostly cigarettes when they won anything at all.

In 1895 Bavarian-born Charles Fey invented the three-reel gambling device, which he called "The Liberty Bell." This became the prototype for the American slot machine. Ten years later, the Nevada legislature recognized the nickel-in-the-slot as the state "bird."

"With all the puff and all the fluff, you have to remember that gambling was illegal in the beginning," says Dan Mead of Mead Publishing Company in Las Vegas. "When you talk about illegal gambling, there were no rules. It was almost like war. There were companies in the thirties that openly manufactured and advertised illegal gambling equipment."

The H. C. Evans Company of Chicago, since defunct, offered a catalog to its customers called "The Secret Blue Book," which promoted such gaff as marked cards and over a dozen different types of loaded dice. Other items available included (1) mirror rings for seeing the faces of the cards while dealing, (2) glasses for reading markings on the backs of cards, (3) guns for quick exits. One ad even offered "Cards...marked, crimped, bent, shaved and shampooed."

Traveling gamblers who used such equipment were known as "crossroaders," or, if caught in the act, as crossed-out crossroaders. Today such things as illegal dice are collector's items. Ask a manufacturer about them and all you get back is a cold stare.

Paul Endy, founder of Paul-Son Gaming Equipment, got into the business during 1952 in California. "At one time," he said, "there was as much gambling in other states, if not more, than in Nevada. They were sneak games ... every club had a poker game, the Elks lodges had slot machines. You have to realize, before the

Kefauver investigations years ago, that all the states had gambling whether it was legal or not."

Endy was manufacturing gambling equipment in a state where gaming was unlawful, so in 1960 he moved his company to Las Vegas. Now he has offices in Reno and Atlantic City, and services casinos in Australia, Germany, Yugoslavia, the Bahamas and the Philippines. "To tell you the truth," he says, "we're so busy trying to get the stuff out that we don't have time to count the number of casinos." The "stuff" includes custom casino furniture, dice, chips, playing cards, layouts, drop boxes, table signs, plastic accessories, slot stands and personalized gambling equipment.

It is a far cry from the early years in Las Vegas, when games of chance were played for everything *except* money. Over each early slot machine was a sign that spelled out the procedure to win mints, gum, free drinks or even music. "Drop one cent in slot, pull knob and let go at once. 4 Aces, 10 Cigars."

One of the most extensive collections of antique slots in the world is on exhibit at the Stardust Hotel in Las Vegas. The "Olde-Tyme Gambling Museum" houses over $3 million worth of machines, according to director Shelley Roberts. Of particular interest is the Guessing Bank, the oldest and one of the smallest machines on display; the "Iron Claws" amusement game; and the old upright coin machines, including the Mills Dewey (worth $50,000) with intricately etched glass on its front that cannot be duplicated even with today's modern technology.

The museum is located at the end of the quarter-mile-long Stardust casino, which was recently remodeled at a cost of $51 million. Stardust Vice President Ralph Purnell says that "in this museum you can literally walk through the history of gambling.'' That is, providing you have enough energy left after hiking a quarter of a mile.

Early slot machines were made entirely of cast iron, and then gradually changed to cast iron fronts with wooden sides. ''The basic design of the three-reel machine has not changed in the last 80 years,'' said Dan Mead, who is publisher of the slot machine monthly ''Loose Change.'' ''The golden age of slots was the 1930s when the machines were very decorative.'' The most valuable slot machine, according to Mead, is the Liberty Bell, built by Fey. His heirs have reportedly turned down bids of up to $75,000 for one of the three Liberty machines still known to exist.

Mead told an interesting story about those early years when gambling for money was illegal. At the time there was a popular brand of gum called Bell, which came in fruit flavors and featured a bar on the wrapper as its trademark. ''Early in this century, when the very first machines were built, gum dispensers were put on the sides of the machines that vended Bell gum. The bar symbol on the slot machine came from the bar on the original wrapper, and the bell was a bonus symbol. The gum came in orange, cherry, plum, and so forth, so consequently those were the other symbols used on the reels. In this business, when you hit on a winning combination you stick with it.'' To evade gambling laws, if a piece of gum was sold with the play it was not looked upon as actual gambling. Coupons were also dispensed in other machines that were redeemable for merchandise.

Mead says that most older slot machines are now used on cruise ships or in special arcades in a few casinos. Video slots are the modern way of ''reeling'' in the players, but it is interesting to note that no longer do the reels on slot machines stop haphazardly as they once did. Instead, a random generator is used that sends an electronic signal to the reel motors. "So today," Mead said, "the number of symbols on a reel doesn't mean anything." As far as video poker is concerned, which is the most popular of the new electronic games, every hand is played with a brand new deck.

Slot machines have reached a new peak of popularity among Las Vegas gamblers — 66,387 handles cranking in 1987 that spewed out about half the city's gaming revenue of 2.4 billion dollars! This breaks down to one slot machine for every 8.58 residents. The average tourist, however, likes pitting his money against a machine because live action at the tables would sometimes frighten even General George Patton.

Because of this popularity, more and more states are allowing its citizens the legal right to have slot machines in their homes. Of course, as Dan Mead says, "Residents of each state should contact their state Attorney General's office and find out specifically what the law in that state is. These laws are constantly changing."

In Montana, slot machines are not allowed on public premises for sale or display, although state residents can play video draw poker. The machines do not have a coin payout hopper, but instead winning tickets are dispensed that are redeemed for cash up to $100. Most states, including Montana, allow a person the right to own a slot machine *if* it is to be used for collecting purposes only, and *if* it will not be used for gambling. In order for the machine to be a collector's item, it usually has to be 25 years old which rules out electronic slots for private owners.

The ages vary from one state to the next, and most state laws are fairly simple. For instance, Missouri says "any machine over 30 years old is presumed to be an antique."

New York: "Any machine manufactured prior to 1950 is presumed to be an antique." In Arizona "any machine manufactured 25 years ago is presumed to be an antique." But then in Virginia "present laws are unclear." In Texas, watch out! "When a slot machine is purchased by a state citizen it is required that within 30 days of purchase the buyer supplies name of machine, year of manufacture, and serial number to local law enforcement agency. Failure to do so is constituted as a *felony*." In other words, if the machine is 30, and you do not report it within 30, then *you* do 30.

Once an individual decides to buy a slot machine, it is a good idea to grab hold of something like the Loose Change Blue Book, which lists the prices of various machines, from Grade 1 (top of the line) to Grade 5. (How'd you get it over here, Chuck, on the back of your skateboard?)

Victor Novelty Works has something called a "Mixed Double" that rates five stars. This baby was built in 1904, when slot machines were slot machines. She's cast iron, so you know she's solid, and I'm gonna let you have her for only thirty thousand. I can see by that look on your face she's out of your price range, but cheer up, I got just what you're looking for. Over here in the corner . . . watch out for that broken glass. . .is your "Chrome Mystery" Diamond-front Escalator Bell, put out by Mills, and she's priced to move fast at only $475. Don't worry about that rattling noise. A little WD-40, and she's as good as new.

The Bantam Reserve Jackpot Ever Full Fancy Front Miniature Escalator Bell is only $1,850, while the Single Jackpot Front Vender Blue Seal Gooseneck Bell Number 52 goes for $2,000. The Watling Baby Gold Award Twin Jackpot Ball Gum Vender Gold Seal Gooseneck Bell Front

Vender is $1750; the Five-Pull Gold Award Cherry Vender Rol-A-Top Escalator Bell Front Vender is $5,600; and a slot machine called the "Puck" is seven hundred.

What makes slot machines a good collector investment is that just about every early American manufacturer, with the exception of Bally, has gone out of business. Mills Novelty Company became Mills Bell-O-Matic, then the TJM Corporation, and now the Mills Distributing Company... but what it distributes is a Japanese solid-state machine. Today Bally remains the number-one slot machine manufacturer, with Sigma Games of Japan and I.G.T. (International Game Technology) close behind.

Dan Mead adds, "Generally, slot machines are the only things that have definite laws in regards to gaming equipment. To my knowledge, I have never heard of anyone running into any problems by having a roulette wheel or a dice table in his home."

With that thought in mind, picture the following scene. It is a Saturday evening, just around twilight, and Ellen and Steve are due any minute. The kids are at the movies, the stereo purrs contentedly in the corner, and the wine is on ice in the den next to the ROULETTE WHEEL. You adjust your black bow tie, casually brush the slacks of your tuxedo, and begin stacking your PERSONALIZED CHIPS on top of your BLACKJACK TABLE while smiling in a rather debonair fashion to your wife, who is dressed as a COCKTAIL WAITRESS. Oh yes, and your brother-in-law is the DEPUTY SHERIFF.

A basic craps table can be bought for $3,800, although the Paul-Son company once built a brass dice table for Jackie Gleason that cost the entertainer $6,000. The "in" thing now, though, is personalized poker chips, and Paul-

Son has supplied them to such stars as Ryan O'Neal and the late Elvis Presley.

Years ago, craps tables were not the big 14-foot monstrosities that abound today. First they were called "blankets," which was exactly what they were. Then came the "end-dealer" tables. There would be a dealer on each end of the table, hence the name, and layouts were not cluttered with proposition bets. After that came the "tub" tables, still used in some smaller Nevada casinos. These were six feet long and utilized only one dealer. As business increased after World War Two, casinos began moving to 10-foot tables with two dealers and a stickman, then 12-foot tables, and now 14-foot models are commonplace.

Dice tables are constructed of a special type of wood grown overseas and shipped to Paul-Son's offshore company. The frame is then layered with formica. Hard woods such as maple, if that is the customer's preference, are used for the chip rails and to cover the rest of the basic structure. Then the rubber bumpers and mirrors are added, and the last step is covering the flat table surface with the craps layout.

Layouts are made up as ordered by each casino. "In this business," Paul-Son owner Paul Endy said, "you can't anticipate an order. One day the casino may want blue layouts, the next day red ones — you never know."

During his early days in Las Vegas, Endy would call on casino owners personally in order to establish his young new company. "Years ago, when we got an order for 40,000 chips we thought we had struck gold. Now an order for a million chips is nothing." His biggest order was for $3 million worth of gaming equipment when Resorts International opened in Atlantic City.

"There used to be a gentleman in Las Vegas who ran

a very successful casino. Every time he saw a dice salesman come in he would say, 'God, there go all the profits.' "

Endy remembers asking an elderly casino owner in Reno for a dice order. The owner rifled through his desk, coming out with half a dozen dice that were so banged up they looked like old baseballs. "Well, I got six," the owner said. "If I don't lose any, I'll be all right for a couple of more months."

Nowadays, with each shift in the casino preferring its own sets of dice, the average order per casino varies from 300 to 1,500 pair per month. A set of dice costs around $2.50 a pair, layouts are $65, and the stick used on the craps table is $24. Playing cards go for 95 cents a pack, and roulette balls are $6 each. One oldtimer tells the story of the time he was running a roulette game in Galveston near an open window of the casino. "I gave that ball a spin and the darn thing flew right out the window into the ocean. It was the only ball we had, and so that was the end of the roulette game."

Gambling chips (or "checks" as they are known in gambling jargon) cost the manufacturer 49 and a half cents each. Endy would not divulge the formula for making his chips. "It has been in the Endy family for 40 years. I will say there has never been a successful attempt to counterfeit our chips." The process requires nine different stages and takes a period of four months to complete. Patterns and designs have to be produced, then the finished product must be approved both by the casino owner and the state gaming commission.

"Counterfeiting is something that keeps us awake a few nights," Endy said. "The sad thing about counterfeiting is that there are very few teeth in the law. All we can do is try to create a product that is protected against counterfeiters. We have to be our own police department, because we're like the U.S. Mint. We have to produce these chips (which are exchangeable for American currency) and we have to give our customer the guarantee that we're not going to duplicate them.''

Consequently, every set of casino chips made by Paul-Son is registered. "If you ordered chips in 1964, I could go back and tell you when you bought them..what color you bought..where we shipped them..back 35 and even 40 years ago. That's why so many casinos have confidence with us.''

To prove his point, Endy told a story about a casino owner who called him on the phone. He had ordered 30,000 $25 chips 30 years before, and now 10,000 of the chips were missing. "I went over and showed the owner his purchase order. He thought for a minute, and then said, 'I remember now, we put those chips in a cabinet and locked them up.' We went upstairs and opened this old dusty cabinet, and the door fell off! The pins had been taken out of the hinges.'' The owner looked around for his accountant, but the bookkeeper had beat such a hasty retreat that his hat and coat were still perched atop his hatrack.

The fact that Paul-Son's five factories are located off-shore gives him more protection against theft. Since it is a federal offense to cross state lines with stolen merchandise, a person will think twice before trying to smuggle chips or any other gambling equipment through customs.

Endy boasts that his accounting procedure is so stringent that thievery is virtually impossible. "Our system,'' he says, "is triple what it would be in a bank.'' The Paul-Son company has to be careful. After all, as Endy himself says, "If all the chips we've made for casinos were stacked end on end we could probably build a freeway around the world.''

The Bud Jones Company of Las Vegas, another large chip manufacturer, has turned out 20 million of them in the last 13 years. More than half of his business is overseas sales, with chips supplied to over 250 casinos in 30 countries. He also holds a patent on the relatively-new "coin-imbedded" chip. One he recently designed was for the Colorado Belle casino in Laughlin, Nevada. "It's red, white and blue with a brass center. It's American. It's flag waving. It's the most beautiful thing we have to offer.''

Jones sees the day coming when his chips can do double duty at the gaming tables and the slot machines. He also predicts that imbedded sensors in chips will be used to monitor both a chip's denomination and its location. For example, if a dealer attempted to leave the pit with an unauthorized chip, the sensor would trip a detector..which would tip an inspector..who would clip the defector.

Meanwhile, the Burt Company in Portland, Maine, has come up with a new design for poker chips that it believes will revolutionize the casino chip industry. Alonzo Burt opened shop in 1895 making pool balls, and 20 years later began stamping out poker chips. The process is a lot like making cookies. . .the "batter" is Texas clay mixed with shellac and dyes, which is melted and pressed out into thin sheets while the chips are cut out by compressed molders.

The Burt Company's new idea is to employ the use of bar codes, the same principle utilized in major grocery stores. Using a bar code scanner, a casino cashier could quickly verify that the chip is not a counterfeit.

The words "new" and "revolutionary" seem to fall on deaf ears in Nevada, however. Tom Sutton, a casino shift boss at Bally's in Las Vegas, said current practices seem to provide adequate protection against counterfeiting. Lee Skelley, games manager at the Las Vegas Hilton, said counterfeiting has been rare in his experience but "it's something to be guarded against." When asked how Caesars Palace guarded itself against counterfeit chips a casino cashier said, "We can tell just by feeling a chip whether it is ours or not."

Something else that has a nice comfortable feel to it is a pair of Las Vegas dice. . . bouncin' lightly in your hand, tiny little rattles as they click a-gin each other. . . reflections of old glory just a-dancin' off dem bones. . . flyin' down the table as the crowd begins to roar, one dice settin' on five and the other. . . on the floor.

When you talk about gambling, nothing says it better. People are always asking pit bosses for dice to take home as souvenirs, and one time they were given away freely. (Not the pit bosses, unfortunately, but the dice.) Then one of the corporation vice-presidents in charge of marketing realized that the dice could be *sold* to gift shops, and the hotel could save up to three hundred dollars a week! The vice-president in charge of marketing sent a memo to the vice-president in charge of casino operations, who sent a memo to the vice-president in charge of vice-presidents, and eventually the decision was made to spit in the eye of any poor soul with the audacity to try to get something for nothing.

At one time dice were made out of a toxic, nauseous substance called nitric celluloid, a nifty little by-product of the petroleum industry. If the Germans had used this stuff in 1945 they could have won the war! When someone working in a plant making dice from this material told his insurance man, his yearly premium was apt to be more than his annual income. In one incident, thirty people died in a factory making dice out of nitric celluloid. It did not actually burn when it caught fire; it exploded.

Dice today burn as slowly as wood, which should make all of us sleep better tonight. Thanks to modern plastics, the whole thing is a cut-and-dried affair. The dice are cut out in rough little cubes, usually five-eighths of an inch in size, from a square sheet of acrylic plastic. These are ground down with a sander, and then the spots are drilled by a micrometer. A syringe fills the holes with a plastic paint that is exactly the same weight as the material it replaced. The dice are then smoothed, and either a polished or lapped surface gives the product the finished touch. After that, the dice are tattooed with the casino's insignia and a series of numbers, usually four digits, which makes it nigh impossible for some unscrupulous player to dupe the house. All of this is a far cry from those days of yesteryear when sheets of nitric celluloid had to be hung in warehouses for nine months and cured like tobacco leaves, just to make one pair of dice.

The secret of a good dice maker, according to Paul Endy, is "making his spots as shallow as possible so there can be no way of inserting weights inside. If you start seeing deep spots in dice, look out."

Owners of gambling casinos are usually superstitious about the dice they use. Endy acknowledges being known as "Passing Paul-Son" by some embittered cronies, suggesting that his dice "pass" too often. But Endy maintains that all dice manufacturers get the same plastic from the same company. One time a pit boss, who was upset with the superstitious nature of the owner, had all of Paul-Son's dice put in wrappers of various other makers. The next day, Endy happened to be walking through the casino and the owner was in a festive mood. He held up a pair of

Endy's own dice, in somebody else's wrapper, and grinned. "See these? We won big last night, and we didn't need you."

Another casino once ordered all its chips with only the name of the club on them. The owner did not feel that denominations were important. "Any idiot knows that $1 chips are blue, $5 chips are red, and $25 are green." Endy said, "Of course, we had to race over there in the middle of the night, pick the chips up in small quantities, and put the denominations on them. It took us two weeks to replace them all."

One casino owner was famous for using cheap material on his casino chairs. When informed that the material he selected would not last six months he replied, "Put it on. We'll cover the chairs with asses."

Of course, with all the jokes and all the funny stories it has to be realized that casino owners are faced with a mounting problem. Everything keeps going up in price, not just the cost of gaming equipment, but also maintenance expenses, wages, insurance, uniforms, and food. The question is how does a *casino* go up? The odds on the various games stay the same, which is why the 14-foot craps table came into being. Instead of accommodating eight players, the table can oblige 14. More people means more revenue. Larger casinos and taller high-rises are the only way to keep up without changing the game's percentages.

"The casinos know how to adapt," Endy ended his interview. "The husband wants to play craps, the wife wants to play poker — they got 'em. The wife wants to play keno, the husband wants to play roulette — they got 'em. Now they've got the sports books. They've got everything for everybody. For a casino to be successful today, you've got to have it all!"

CHAPTER 6

Law and Order

QUESTION: Can a casino legally change the dice in the middle of a hand at a craps game?

ANSWER: There is no statute or regulation that prohibits a casino from doing this. However, if the Gaming Control Board determines that the dice switching was "for illegal purposes," the licensee might be subject to disciplinary action pursuant to Regulation 5.011, and those involved would be subject to criminal prosecution.

QUESTION: Can a casino legally bar a proficient gambler from playing?

ANSWER: Yes. Players commonly known as "card counters" may legally be barred from a casino. Gaming statutes and regulations in the state of Nevada are silent on this issue, unless there is evidence of cheating.

QUESTION: What would happen if a gangster was discovered on the premises of a Las Vegas resort?

ANSWER: Disciplinary action, up to and including closure, could be instituted against any establishment... pursuant to Regulation 5.011.5. "Catering to, assisting, employing or associating with...persons of notorious or

unsavory reputation or who have extensive police records
. . . is grounds for license revocation."

In 1974, the Duncs Hotel was fined $10,000 after reput-
ed Kansas City crime figure Nick Civella was provided with
complimentary services for six days. In the early 1960s,
entertainer Frank Sinatra gave up his state gaming license
after "rolling out the red carpet" for the late Sam Gian-
cana, reputed Chicago mob boss. At the time, Sinatra was
a major stockholder of the Cal-Neva Club at Lake Tahoe
and also held a nine percent ownership in the Las Vegas
Sands Hotel.

Sinatra was later licensed as a key employee of Caesars
Palace by the Nevada Gaming Commission. "Having your
picture taken with someone," said the commission chairman, "or attending parties with mobsters. . . should not
rule out someone for a license."

QUESTION: Can a casino legally close a slot machine
(or blackjack game) after a player has won a considerable
amount of money?

ANSWER: There is nothing which prohibits a casino
from closing any game or slot machine, nor is there any
prohibition against a casino changing dealers in the case
of table games. It is important to note that casino games
and devices are considered games of chance which involve
randomness and statistical probabilities. If the rules are
consistent, a player has the same probability of winning
(or losing) regardless of the dealer or table.

With respect to slot machines, it is not uncommon for
a casino to temporarily shut down a slot machine after a
series of wins in order to inspect the machine for malfunc-
tions or tampering. In the case of large progressive slot
machines, a casino may elect to permanently remove those

devices once the jackpot is won. However, a progressive jackpot must remain available to the public until won. (Regulation 5.110)

Regardless of the question, there is an answer in the 872-page Nevada Gaming Commission regulations manual. This inch-thick handbook is the commission's bible, and the commission's disciples are the members of the Gaming Control Board. The policy of both the commission and the board, the handbook states, is "to require that all establishments wherein gaming is conducted be operated in a manner suitable to protect...the general welfare of the inhabitants of the state."

For the first 14 years that gambling was legal in Nevada, there was no such thing as a regulations manual or, for that matter, a state gaming agency of any kind. Thievery was so wide-spread in some casinos that a Las Vegas bar advertised: "Attention, Dealers. Cash Your Tokes Here. We Pay 80 Cents On The Dollar!"

Rumor has it that a pit boss in one gambling hall was caught cheating during that turbulent era. The man was taken downstairs to the hotel's basement, stripped of his clothing, and handcuffed to an overhead water pipe. He hung there for two days, where he was used as a punching bag by the owner and his sons. Fortunately for the pit boss, the owner's wife found out about it, and the man was reluctantly released. The oldtimer who told the story said, "He was one guy you never asked about the good old days."

It was 1946, the only moment in time when what happened in Las Vegas could have occurred at all. People were tired of reading about housing shortages and Iron Curtains and a frightening new invention called the A-bomb.

Something mad and foolish was happening close to home, in an offbeat wild west town just down the road from L.A. A hood named Bugsy Siegel was building a gambling joint with the mob's money, and it touched that little spot of reckless abandon inside all of us.

Siegel was smooth. He was rakishly handsome...he was tough...and he had connections. With the war over, building materials were at a premium, yet Siegel's Flamingo Hotel shot up in eight short months. Never mind that it cost him three times what he figured on spending, or rumors that he was funneling most of the money out of the country. This $6 million resort would put Vegas on the map. It might not put Bugsy in the White House, but at least it would keep him out of the doghouse.

The Flamingo opened December 26, 1946. Siegel leaned back with his hands in his pockets and jawed with reporters. "What you see here today is nothing," he said. "More and more people are moving to California every day, and they love to gamble. In ten years, this'll be the biggest gambling center in the world."

He wound up batting five hundred. He was right about the future of Las Vegas, wrong about the future of Bugsy Siegel. Six months later, he was gunned down in his girlfriend's apartment.

While all of this was going on, Wilbur Clark was running around the country trying to get financial backing for a resort he wanted to build in Las Vegas. It would be a combination hotel and country club, with 300 rooms and a golf course. Clark got the money, and the Desert Inn opened in 1950. He also got some unsavory partners, which brought him an invitation to appear before the Kefauver Crime Committee in Washington:

Senator Charles Tobey:	"Before you got into bed with crooks to finish this proposition, didn't you look into these birds at all?"
Wilbur Clark:	"Not too much. No sir."
Sen. Tobey:	"You have a smile on your face, but I don't know how the devil you do it."
Clark:	"I have done it all my life."

That was all the Desert Inn needed. Wilbur Clark was suddenly "in" with the "Inn" crowd, and the first year the hotel was open it made a staggering $2 million profit. Not to be outdone, other entrepreneurs poured into Las Vegas. . .and by 1955 there were ten major resorts on the Strip.

Promoter Anthony Stralla decided it was time to make his move. Stralla, alias Tony Cornero, was a professional gambler with big ideas and a five-figure bank account: $375.95. There was a vacant piece of land just across the Strip from the splashy new Riviera, and it was the perfect spot for a new casino. All Cornero needed to make his dream come true was $10 million. He raised the money by selling stock to investors, keeping 50 percent ownership. The only thing Cornero neglected to do was register his company with the Securities and Exchange Commission, and this put the new hotel into bankruptcy even before it opened.

Cornero died in 1955, and the property was sold to John Factor, brother of cosmetics baron Max Factor. Factor leased it to Moe Dalitz, who was one of the financial backers of the Desert Inn, and in 1958 the Stardust Hotel finally opened.

Dalitz was a shrewd businessman with a questionable past. He grew up in Detroit, where he was a boyhood chum of future Teamsters Union leader Jimmy Hoffa. He sold bootleg whiskey during Prohibition, and later ran illegal gambling joints in the Midwest. Dalitz wanted to make the Stardust the largest resort in the world, so he expanded the hotel in 1964 to 1,400 rooms. He got the money to do so ($7 million) by going to his old pal Hoffa at the Teamsters Union.

In 1968, the Stardust — and its debts — were acquired by the Parvin-Dohrmann Corporation, which also owned the Fremont Hotel. Delbert Coleman, chairman of the company, kept the property for six years, and then sold it to Allen Glick of the Argent Corporation. Glick, a San Diego real estate investor, already owned the Hacienda and Marina Hotels, and got the money to buy the Stardust by going to the Teamsters Union.

There was a catch, though. Glick was to keep a certain individual on the Stardust payroll, a man by the name of Frank Rosenthal. Glick would own the Stardust; Rosenthal would run it. Glick was in a a tight spot. Rosenthal, known as "Lefty" by his associates, had once been fined $6,000 for trying to fix a college basketball game. He had been indicted on charges of running an illegal sports betting operation. His circle of friends included reputed mobsters who had arranged Glick's loan from the Teamsters. Like it or not, Rosenthal was suddenly Glick's right-hand man.

Rosenthal, who was only a blackjack floorman when Glick took over the Stardust, became "executive corporate consultant" of the hotel. An uneasy truce between the two prevailed until Rosenthal was denied licensing as a key employee by the Nevada Gaming Commission. It was then that longtime Las Vegas gamer Carl Thomas was introduced to Glick by Teamsters lawyer Allan Dorfman. Dorfman told Glick that Thomas was temporarily being put in charge at the Stardust. Glick, who had already been threatened by Rosenthal's associates, did not argue.

Thomas was casino manager at Circus Circus in the early 1970s, during which time the hotel had borrowed money for a new high rise from the Teamsters Union. He later testified that he was given an ownership share in the business by consenting to run a skim operation. This practice was continued at the Stardust, with Thomas later quoted as saying, "It was like having a bucket with 20 holes going every way. No control. Money was pouring out."

Race book employees were writing tickets after the events were over; slot machine personnel were making out false jackpot tickets; the hotel prepaid its advertising and received kickbacks under the table; fill-slips were forged on the gaming tables; electronic scales were miscalibrated so that extra money could be siphoned off.

On the night of May 18, 1976, gaming agents raided the Stardust. They discovered a secret bank inside the hotel containing $10,000; "perhaps a day's skim," one investigator said afterwards. State gaming officials estimated the total casino skim was close to $20 million, and Allen Glick was called before the Nevada Gaming Commission. His gaming license was revoked and Argent was fined $700,000. Glick was given 18 months to sell out.

Glick leased his casinos to Trans-Sterling, a company formed by former Stardust manager Al Sachs. Sachs would buy Argent outright three years later for $68 million, while Glick — who was never charged with any wrongdoing — retreated to a $6 million estate in California. Sadly, old habits are hard to break, and a state complaint in 1983 charged Sachs and partner Herb Tobman with "failing to properly investigate or take appropriate action to determine if skimming occurred" at the Stardust. In 1982 alone, $1.4 million was allegedly skimmed off the tables by a group of Stardust executives — with the "chief mechanics" of the operation being identified as the casino manager and assistant casino manager.* Although not admitting their guilt, Sachs and Tobman gave up their gaming licenses. They also paid a $3 million fine, the largest in state history, and the Stardust was taken over by the widely-respected Boyd hotel group.

Unethical casino practices, however, have plagued the state of Nevada since gambling was legalized in 1931. Gaming control at that time was the responsibility of local and county officials, whose main concern was collecting license fees. Then in 1945, a new concept in licensing was introduced by the state legislature. Fees would be based on a percentage of gross winnings, and would be collected by the Nevada Tax Commission. The bill was strictly a revenue measure, and one small point was overlooked. Nothing was ever said about who would *police* the casinos. Sure, some of the owners had nasty reputations outside the state, but what they did in Nevada was strictly legitimate. Besides, if Nevada chased away the only people who knew how to operate gambling casinos, it would have toppled the state's primary industry.

When the Nevada Gaming Control Board was created in 1955, it found itself in a dilemma. Set up within the Tax Commission, the board was given the task of weeding out casino undesirables while trying to keep revenues up. It did not help matters when Meyer Lansky's brother was

---

*SOURCE: Nevada Gaming Control Board vs. Trans-Sterling, Inc., dba Stardust; Allan D. Sachs; and Herbert L. Tobman. Case Number 83-10, Dec. 8, 1983.

found to be a hidden owner of the Thunderbird in 1955, or that gambling statistics from the Tropicana were found in the pocket of mobster Frank Costello two years later. What had begun as a unique American dream was mushrooming into a full-blown nightmare.

Thus in 1959, the whole system was restructured with the passage of the Gaming Control Act. This established the Nevada Gaming Commission to work alongside the Gaming Control Board, which was removed from the Tax Commission. (A third board, the Gaming Policy Committee, was set up in 1961 to make non-binding recommendations concerning gaming policy.)

It sounds complicated, but Gaming Control Board member Dennis Amerine untangled it in a broad-ranging interview:

"The three members of the Gaming Control Board work full-time for the state, and we are considered the investigative arm of the entire regulatory system. The Gaming Commission, on the other hand, is made up of five individuals who work on a part-time basis. They are the final authority on recommendations that we make for licensing."

Amerine started as an agent with the Control Board's Audit Division in 1977, was named chief of that division eight years later, then was appointed by the governor to a four-year term on the Control Board itself in 1987. "It was not what you would consider a normal job for an auditor," he recalled. "I remember sitting outside of a casino at about 3 a.m. with binoculars, inside of a van, looking to see when one of the owners was going to drop some of the drop boxes from which we thought he was stealing. It was quite hysterical, seeing a couple of accountants right out of college, trying to do covert surveillance. Things have become a little more sophisticated since then."

In order to properly perform all its functions, the Gaming Control Board maintains a staff of more than 300 in various divisions:

Investigations Agents from this division do a thorough background check on any applicant seeking a state gaming license. It requires agents to travel extensively, but taking a dreary old plane ride to Paris or London is just one of the hazards of the job. The applicant bears the entire cost of the investigation anyway, and the money is not refunded even if no license is granted. "It can be a very complicated investigation when you go into a foreign country," Amerine said. "There's the language barrier, for example. Volumes and volumes of financial information have to be translated." That is one reason why it took nine agonizing months to license Ginji Yasuda at the Aladdin.

Special Investigations And Intelligence "This is our liaison with the FBI and other law enforcement agencies," Amerine revealed. The division, with a long list of informants, investigates such non-routine gaming problems as hidden casino ownership and organized crime involvement in Nevada casinos.

Audit This division is responsible for the audit of casino operations and the enforcement of gaming regulations. In the past, this caused a lot of friction between gaming control authorities and the two major groups which represented Nevada casinos: the Gaming Industry Association in northern Nevada, and the Nevada Resorts Association in southern Nevada. "Much of it was caused by such things as (our) adopting regulations and implementing industry-wide requirements without industry input," Amerine said. "In recent years, however, we have been able to work together in adopting regulations which are satisfactory to both the regulators and the industry.'' A good example of this new-found harmony was the passage of the revised Regulation 6, which deals with casino revenue controls. The Audit Division of the board worked for over two years with the NRA and other industry representatives before the regulation was finally implemented. Still, Nevada resorts have to toe the line. ''The Audit Division will go into each hotel at least two or three times a year on a surprise basis,'' Amerine said.

Tax and License and Economic Research This division is charged with the collection and accounting of all tax and license fees. Any proposed changes in gaming taxes or fees are sent to Economic Research for further study on how it will affect the industry as a whole.

Enforcement The law enforcement arm of the Gaming Control Board, agents from this division are responsible for the enforcement of all regulations. ''They're out in the field on a regular basis,'' Amerine explained. ''They make routine observations, go undercover when a tip is received, and look for cheaters. Slot machine cheats are one of our biggest problems. In a recent year, Nevada casinos turned in nine *tons* of slugs people had put in slot machines.''

That brings up an interesting point. When is somebody actually cheating at a game of chance, and when is he just using devilish ingenuity? Sticking slugs in a slot machine is one thing, but other cases are still being decided in courts of law. In 1985, a blackjack player was arrested at the Westward Ho casino in Las Vegas after security guards saw him ''exhibiting suspicious body movements.''

It turned out the player had a tiny card-counting microcomputer strapped to his leg, controlled by switches he manipulated with his feet. Tapping his toes, he was able to tell the computer which cards from the deck had been played. The computer then sent back messages advising him how to play his hand by delivering little electric shocks to the rear strap of his athletic supporter! He was arrested for cheating, but filed a lawsuit saying his rights (among other things) had been violated. The argument of the Nevada Resorts Association was that "impeding the transfer of information from one's toes to one's buttocks hardly rates as an infringement of the First Amendment." The case was "assessed" in court and the player lost.

Another gambler once decided to loosen up a slot machine by squirting oil into the coin acceptor. When he pulled the handle, the door of the machine blew off, sending him to the hospital. He was treated for cuts and bruises, then returned to the casino. He wanted his cup of nickels back, which had been on top of the machine he was trying to cheat.

Two elderly women from Phoenix read a newspaper story about a slot cheating method called "stringing." (String, or wire, is attached to a coin through a small hole, and the coin is yo-yoed until it triggers the machine's acceptance switch.) The women made their "yoyo" of bright orange yarn, taping the yarn to the coin as they excitedly went to work. If they lost the coin in the machine, they simply made up a new one. When apprehended by control board agents, the two were astonished. They said they had read about it in the newspapers, for goodness sakes, so how could it be illegal?

The dusty files of the Gaming Control Board are full of documented cases that make these two gals from Arizona look like a couple of den mothers. A stroll down memory lane would not be complete without mentioning the following Nevada establishments, realizing of course that things do change over the years — new owners or new managers, for example, who can set a new course and repair the old image of their operations.

October, 1967. Incline Village Casino, Lake Tahoe. An employee was seen putting loaded dice into play on one of the craps tables. Four more sets were found on his person. The gaming license of the club's owners was suspended for one year.

July, 1968. Pioneer Club, Las Vegas. An incomplete deck of cards was found in play at a blackjack game. In other words, most of the tens hitting the table came from the customers and had Alexander Hamilton's picture on them. The owner was fined $10,000, and the club was permitted to reopen with slot machines only. Since that time, the Pioneer has been sold to new owners.

April, 1966. Silver Nugget, Las Vegas. Female 21 dealers were found to be wearing transparent clothing. The Gaming Control Board saw through it and ordered the owner to "attire all personnel employed in any gaming capacity in decent, modest and proper apparel."

August, 1967. Riverside Resort and Casino, Laughlin. An employee set off a bomb at the residence of a patron who had incurred gambling debts, and also threw another bomb at pursuing police officers. The casino was ordered to have a uniformed security guard on premises, and no further credit was to be issued to any customer at that time.

June, 1972. Churchill Downs Sports Book, Las Vegas. Betting slips were being rewritten after the events in question were over. The owner was fined $10,000, plus $43 for cost of proceedings. In 1981, Churchill Downs was fined another $12,500 after accepting telephone wagers on sporting events.

September, 1986. Churchill Downs again. This time the respondent destroyed safekeeping deposit envelopes and failed to maintain complete, accurate and legible records . . . violating regulations 6.025, 6.020, 6.050, 22.050. The owner was fined $30,000, and the sports book eventually was closed.

October, 1977. Felix's Bank Club, Lovelock. An employee was observed dealing from a cooler deck, "a deck prearranged in sequential fashion so as to alter the normal random selection of criteria which determine the result of the game." The club's license was revoked, and the owner fined $17,500.

November, 1977. TJ's Dirty Bird Casino, Winnemucca. Cheating was observed in a 21 game involving "slugging" by the dealer, "dealing from a deck containing an abnormal distribution of 10-value cards." A lethal weapon, commonly known as a "blackjack," was also found on the premises. (If a player got a blackjack, there was a good chance he was going to get *another* blackjack, this one alongside his head.) Gaming licenses at the appropriately-named club were revoked, and the owners were fined $12,000.

March, 1979. Aladdin Hotel, Las Vegas. The hotel's licensees were charged with numerous violations, including hidden ownership interests. A $200,000 fine was levied against the owners, and their gaming licenses were revoked. The hotel was shut down briefly in 1980, and later reopened under new owners.

July, 1979. Tropicana Hotel, Las Vegas. The officers of the hotel were charged with allowing Joseph Agosto to maintain a secret role in its operation. A Gaming Control Board document stated, ''Inasmuch as Agosto has been the subject of a 20-year effort by Federal authorities to deport... because of his connections with organized crime, and that he was named as an organized crime figure by the California Organized Crime Commission Report.'' Fines eventually amounted to $472,000, and the hotel was sold to the Ramada Corporation.

February, 1979. The Desert Inn, Las Vegas. A reputed New Jersey bookmaker (one Anthony Caputo) was issued credit without proper identification. The bookmaker got away with $524,000, and the hotel was fined another $75,000.

March, 1981. Sahara Hotel, Las Vegas. A reputed New Jersey bookmaker (one Anthony Caputo again) was issued credit without ID, leaving unpaid debts of approximately $520,000.

March, 1981. Sahara Reno. A reputed New Jersey bookmaker (guess who?) made off with $260,000 after getting credit without ID. The two hotels were fined a total of $40,000.

October, 1985. Gary Austin's Race and Sports Book, Las Vegas. A surprise audit by the Gaming Control Board showed a cash deficiency of almost $430,000. The respondent's gaming license was revoked.

February, 1982. Cloud's Cal Neva Lodge, Crystal Bay.

Dennis Amerine of the Gaming Control Board tells the story. "Mr. Cloud first got into trouble when the enforcement division went in and inspected some of his (gambling) devices. They found that some of the star-reels on the slot machines had been shaved off. What this did was change the randomness of each device's performance, or what amounted to a method of cheating the public. He was fined $325,000 and given a limited license as a result of that action.

"That was the first time we ran into problems with Mr. Cloud. Then we went in there a year and a half later and did a thorough audit, and found some very serious internal control problems. We came across information that there may have been a card mechanic working there, so we started a full-fledged investigation. We learned that Mr. Cloud had signed somebody's American Express voucher without authorization, using it to repay a patron's outstanding markers. There were allegations of drugs being sold on the premises, and prostitution...you name it, we found violations. He was not given another license."

Not only does the Gaming Control Board serve as the state's watchdog against unscrupulous casino practices, but it also makes the final decision on table game changes. For instance, Caesars Tahoe has proposed letting blackjack players bet on whether or not their first two cards will be over or under 13. The game variation, invented by pit supervisor Ken Perrie, gives the house an edge of 8.6%, although that is not what makes it so attractive. "Instead of more volume," Perrie explained, "we get more money from the customers we already have." The side game is already being tested, on a trial basis, at the Lake Tahoe casino.

Another game change, already in use at Bob Stupak's Vegas World, is "crapless craps." If a shooter rolls a craps on his first roll (aces, ace-deuce or twelve) he does not lose, but has to roll that same number again before rolling a seven. In exchange for this "privilege," the shooter does not win if he rolls an eleven on his first roll. . . which is an automatic winner in every other casino.

The Control Board also tests new concepts in slot machines, before such devices are unloaded on the public. Caesars Palace recently got approval from the board to use video poker machines with the instructions and wording printed in Spanish. On these bilingual coin-guzzlers, a royal flush is *flux royal,* four of a kind is *cuatro de la misma* and a full house is *pierna mas par.* Best of all, payoffs are not in pesos, but in good old *dinero de Americano.*

A machine such as this has to pass a rigid examination before finding its way onto the casino floor. With 62 slot machine manufacturers and distributors licensed in the state of Nevada, the control board's engineers and technicians stay busy checking the intentions of brand new inventions. Said Dennis Amerine, "We've had devices submitted that were more like carnival games, and don't belong in a casino atmosphere."

Here is the route a new machine must take. First, it is submitted for laboratory testing for a period of up to four months, depending on the quality of the device. Testing is done using computer simulators, with thousands upon thousands of plays made to check its overall performance. Modifications are recommended if necessary. Then, the device is placed on the board and commission's agenda for field trial consideration, usually for a period of 60 days. After the field trial is concluded, the device goes back on the agenda for final approval. The factors that decide a new machine's fate are its security features (to prevent players from cheating the casinos); its randomness and hit frequency (to prevent casinos from cheating the players); and its reliability (to prevent the device from malfunctioning while it is preventing everyone from cheating everyone).

A former slot machine manufacturer did not mince words as he explained his version of the lengthy process. "The board will test the machine thoroughly, all at the manufacturer's expense. This can be very, very costly if you're a newcomer and the competition doesn't like you. Or it can be a very simple operation if you're somebody who has contributed greatly to the state of Nevada. I look at the whole situation as 90 percent political and ten percent needed. Then when a machine is finally tested to the board's satisfaction, and the limits of your expense, the board will either approve it or disapprove it...or allow it to be operated in a location for a certain period of time to see how it works out."

That raises the next question. Are Nevada slot manufacturers on friendly terms with the Control Board? "We attempt to maintain a good working relationship with all licensees," Amerine said. If a slot manufacturer or distributor violates any gaming regulation, it could mean either a fine or the revocation of the company's license.

Nevada Electronics was fined $20,000 in 1967 for installing circuitry in its blackjack machines to produce low-value cards on the first "hit" sequence. Centaur Mini Devices lost its license in 1975 for transporting slot machines and/or parts thereof across state lines. Casino Coin Machine Operators lost its license in 1977 for not filing financial statements to the Control Board. The Antique Gambler lost its license in 1984 for shipping slot machines to a phony address outside Nevada.

One device recently approved by the Gaming Control Board is "Auto Roulette," an automated machine one-third the size of a standard roulette table. Developed by Games of Nevada, this gadget features touch-betting on every conceivable bet offered at a live game. . . and even has a real ball whizzing around a real wheel.

The Status Game Corporation plans to open a casino in Henderson with nothing but video games. Owner Irv Yaffa says, "It will have video craps, poker, blackjack, keno, bingo — just about every video game that's out. It's easier to control, and a lot less expensive in terms of payroll." A well-known Las Vegas casino boss got accolades from the press (and hand grenades from his employees) when he said, "Slot machines are the wave of the future. They do not require uniforms, meals, hospitalization, or other benefits. . . and they work 24 hours a day without complaining."

On the other hand, Maxim casino host Russell Scott says, "There's not enough incentive at this point to drag people here just to play machines." Someday slot machines may rule the gaming industry, but the former Desert Inn casino manager said, "It won't happen in our lifetime."

Wherever the road may take us, gambling in Nevada is big business. A lot of people still make a lot of money. Kids have good schools, their parents have good jobs, and millions of tourists have a good time. And if they lose their money while they are doing it, at least they did it "fair and square."

Stated simply in the Nevada Gaming Commission's regulations manual (Reg. 4.010.2):

"An application for a license, determination of

suitability, or registration, besides any other factor attaching to such an application by virtue of the Nevada Gaming Control Act and the regulations thereunder, shall constitute a request to the board and commission for a decision upon the applicant's general suitability, character, integrity, and ability to participate or engage in, or be associated with, the gaming industry in the manner or position sought by the applicant, or the manner or position generally similar thereto; and, by filing an application with the board, the applicant specifically consents to the making of such a decision by the board and commission at their election when the application, after filing, becomes moot for any reason other than death.''

It couldn't be said any better.

CHAPTER 7

Professional Gamblers

The guys were sitting around the table swapping yarns. Cigar smoke hung in the air like river fog, and a person had to squint to see across the room.

"One day my whole family was playing cards — even my two-year-old granddaughter. I said, 'Well, that's really great. I didn't think she'd learn to play poker this fast.' My daughter said, 'She's not as smart as she looks. She's lost four hands in a row.' "

Jack "Treetop" Straus heehawed as he told the story, but when professional poker players get together someone always has a topper. It is almost like, "I'll see that one and raise you."

Doyle Brunson cleared his throat. "This guy named Lowball Pete went over to his friend Shorty's house and Pete said to Shorty: 'I've got to have some money, the baby don't have any food, the rent's due, and they're going to throw me out of the house.' So Shorty, who was a good friend of Pete's, said: 'Well, I understand, here's $100.' Pete said: 'Thanks, Shorty, I'll pay you back as soon as I can.' Shorty said: 'Well, I know that. Where are you going now?' And Pete said: 'I'm going over to Al's house, they have a $200 limit lowball game going.' Shorty said:

'Well, what difference does that make, how are you going to play?' And Pete said, 'Oh, I've got money for *that*!' "

Stories like this usually come during dry spells in a poker game. Then the guys will get down to business, and things go quiet. There is no music in the background, no tinkly laughter, just the constant clatter of poker chips being nervously riffled by the players . . . and an occasional grunt as somebody sees or somebody calls. Other than that, there is just cold heavy silence.

Then a big hand will end, and people start breathing again. "If I'd of bet two hundred, you might not have called it," Johnny Moss said, raking in the pot. The other man's lips went tight, but he threw in his ante for the next hand. The others at the table followed suit, and the dealer started shuffling.

Poker players are a rare breed, rough and tumble throwbacks from the old Wild West and Mississippi riverboats. Who can ever forget Wild Bill Hickok and his aces and eights, the last beautiful sight he beheld before exiting Deadwood? Or Joe Bernstein, who never sat down to a game without wearing a tie.

The game of poker is the ultimate contest. It makes stars out of ordinary people, and every star has a nickname: Treetop, Texas Dolly, The Kid, Amarillo Slim, The Cowboy, The Grand Old Man.

The Grand Old Man is Johnny Moss, now in his 80s and a member of the prestigious Poker Hall of Fame. Talking with Moss is like flying at night without instruments. He is liable to take a conversation anywhere, but the trip is filled with wit and nostalgia. Asked if it were possible for anyone to make a living as a professional poker player, he leaned back and here it came:

"Sure, if they're not being cheated. Years ago there were

so many cheaters —''

But not now.

"Naw, they got good protection."

So could a person nowadays play poker and make a living at it?

"Oh yeah, they were doing a little cheating around when I come out here to Vegas. I broke it up. See, I had a poker game, had twelve tables at the Dunes. You know what I had up on the wall? 'I Take Half The Pot.' Fifty percent take off. If there was 400 in the pot, I'd take 200. I had a sign up. A local would come in there and they'd complain about it. I'd say, 'Get the hell out of here.' First I had a 25 percent sign, but my dealers was taking more than that, so I put up a 50 percent sign. Then they took more than *that*, and I got in trouble."

Moss left the Dunes, but in 1981 hotel owner Morris Shenker asked him to take the poker room back. "I don't want it back," Moss said. "Why don't you take it back and work for me?" Shenker asked him. "What are you gonna pay me?" Moss countered. "I'll pay you $100,000 a year; give you room, board, and laundry; and pay your wife $50,000 a year." Moss got home and broke the news to his wife. She said to him, "Have you been going around looking for work?" He answered, "Naw, I was getting *you* a job."

Moss lives in a suite at the Golden Nugget now, and every December he is practically the trail boss in the Nugget's Grand Prix of Poker. He has played in nearly a hundred tournaments since 1970, finishing in the money an amazing 13 times. "Tournaments killed poker," he says. "Everbody plays in tournaments. See, I was a good tournament player. I guess I won as many tournaments as anybody." He is not exaggerating. Across the street at the

Horseshoe Club, he took the World Series of Poker championship three times.

Johnny Moss is the best at what he does, which is making a living as a professional gambler. If you do not believe it, just ask him.

He went up two chest sizes as he said, "I'm still the best player in the world, playing six and seven hours. Everbody's done told me that. I'd like to quit, but there's a game you can't quit. People *give* you their money! In four years I won more money than most people make in a lifetime."

Another member of the Poker Hall of Fame is Puggy Pearson, who says the best hand he ever had was "whatever it took to win. I stole one of the biggest pots I ever won. I was playing heads-up (one on one) with this guy, and we must have had three or four hundred thousand in this pot. I had $1,700 left and I raised him. He folded, laid his cards down face-up, and I had the worst hand. So you talk about best hands. Best hands is what you win with. It don't make no difference what it is."

Pearson came from a large family, a "full house" one might say, with nine brothers and sisters. "And every time the rent come due, we had to move." He scuffled around, shined shoes, hustled pool, went in the Navy when he was 16, started playing poker, and never quit.

The question was posed to Puggy. Could a person make a living today as a professional poker player?

"It's probably the easiest thing in the world to do. I mean, there's nothing no easier than gambling. All you gotta do is know three basic things: when you got the best of it, then you gotta money-manage, and then the toughest thing of all is managing yourself. If you know those three things, you're gonna be a success, just like in any other business you own or operate.'' Puggy aimed his half-foot cigar at an ashtray. ''You're your own business, and sometimes your own worst enemy.''

Pearson was dressed in white, his shirt pockets crammed with notebooks, eyeglasses, sunglasses, ballpoints, and an eight-hour supply of El Ropos. Roosting jauntily on his head was a captain's cap, of course. When complimented on being one of the country's top poker players, he rares like a skittish colt. ''Not one of the top poker players, *the* top,'' he crows. ''The Ayatollah!''

Pearson does not like poker tournaments, but prefers playing in side games. ''Tournaments today are for people with a leather ass who can sit there all day and throw their hand away. A gambler can't do that. I'm an imagination player, I like to bluff, and in these tournaments sooner or later I'm gonna bluff my chips off.''

Asked about his life as a professional gambler, Pearson will say, ''It's the most depressing racket in the world. You win 18 or 19 times in a row, accumulating a big bankroll, then turn around and lose once and you're back where you started. Or you're broke. Then you gotta go out and look for a friendly face and borrow some money, and try to get up off the ground again. I've been there a million times.

''I've been King Kong and the boss of the poker around here for 30 years, and now I'm 60 years old. There's all these punks coming up, they think fast and they're witty. It's hard to keep up with them.

''Playing poker is like being an entertainer, like getting the stage. You got to get control of the people around the table. Then you can lead 'em and drive 'em. You can make 'em call you, make 'em throw their hand away. That's the object of a professional poker player when he sits down at the table, to be able to get control of the game.''

There is no doubt that tournament play is enhancing the popularity of poker. A recent tournament at the Horse-shoe attracted nearly 2,000 contestants, mostly from other states where poker is legal — California, Oregon, Washington and Montana. Surprisingly, poker is *not* legal in Atlantic City casinos, but then again Atlantic City did not even want slot machines in the beginning.

Meanwhile, the times they are a-changing. Every major tournament — and there are eight each year in Nevada — has a separate competition for the fairer sex. The second-ranked money winner on the ladies poker circuit is Las Vegan Cheryl Davis, who says playing poker is ''an easy way to make a tough living.'' She is young, attractive, and unmarried. ''No one will have me as a wife,'' she says, ''but I enjoy this.'' Cheryl had just won $13,500 in a Lady-7 Stud Tournament, subsisting while she played on candy bars and aspirins. ''Everybody applauded for me,'' she said, ''because I owe them all money.''

Cheryl was raised around gambling, and gamblers. . . and found herself attracted to both. ''I never wanted to amount to anything, and it worked out real good.'' She laughed, and then turned more serious. ''I don't know, I guess I liked the spirit of the people, their attitudes. You meet a lot of sleaze-balls, but overall it's a pretty interesting group of people. You can teach a monkey to play cards, but the intuitiveness and the psychology of the moves — being able to read people — is what I enjoy.''

She should be good at it. Cheryl has been playing poker since she was 16, or almost half of her life. ''Things have changed,'' she reflects. ''A woman can go into a card room and not get hit on or railroaded. It used to be just a few of us, but now there are more and more women coming into the poker world. It's really not any different from somebody who goes to work from nine to five. It's a job, and poker now is revolutionized to mostly tournaments. I like tournaments, because if you take 500 and sit down in a side game and win 1,500, that's a good win. But if you take 500 and win a hundred thousand in a tournament, that's a lot better.''

Cheryl was asked the same question. Could somebody else make a go of it playing poker? She thought for a moment, and it was hard to believe this wisp of a girl could hold her own with the likes of Treetop and Pug and the Grand Old Man. ''It takes a certain breed of person. That type of person has to understand that there is no security, and they don't get a gold watch at the end of twenty years. They don't have any health benefits, and they're not going to know what they make from day to day. If they're looking for something that's going to guarantee them $500 a week, they better keep their jobs.''

Of course, playing cards for a living is not for everyone, not even a professional poker player. For eight years, Jack Keller made his living at it. All told, he earned over a million dollars before throwing in his last hand. He said he felt burnt out, and that he did not want his sons to make it three of a kind. So what is he doing now? He's playing the stock market in Chicago!

There is another way to eke out a living at the card tables, according to Dan Mead, editor of *Loose Change* Magazine. ''The only (other) game you can legally make money at is blackjack, the reason being that as a deck of cards is dealt the odds are constantly changing. They change according to whether the deck is rich in ten-count cards or whether it's poor in ten-count cards. There are a number of systems to keep a running count, the most popular being a plus and minus system. You bet heavily when the deck is rich in blackjack hands, and bet lightly otherwise. Indeed, one of my daughters, who was ten years old at the time, learned to apply card counting methods to improve her blackjack game at home.''

The popularity of blackjack is hard to fathom, yet the average Las Vegas tourist allots 23 hours of gambling time to playing it.* The drawback to blackjack is that a player must make his bet before seeing his hand. This gives the casino a decided advantage, or did until card counters arrived on the scene. Casinos hate them, security guards bully them, pit bosses sneer at them, skeptics laugh at them, dealers intimidate them. Why, they have turned a light-hearted sport into a cold cunning science, with the unmitigated gall of knocking the house edge down to a slightly *minus* percent. The nerve of these people!

Author John Gollehon simplified the whole matter of card counting in his books, *Pay The Line* and *Casino Games*. "Little cards help the dealer, and larger cards help the player." Using a count system, he wrote, a card counter will adjust the size of his bets *and* adjust his basic strategy.

This is what gives the counter his advantage over the house. If a deck is fat with high cards, the counter is gambling that he will get more of them than the dealer does. The late Ken Uston claimed to have made a comfortable living as a card counter, but finally had to resort to wearing disguises to stay in action.

Card counting, though, almost has a stigma attached to it. The subject even rated two pages in the book *Gambling Scams*, written by Darwin Ortiz, who is called America's leading authority on crooked gambling. He

*Las Vegas Visitor Profile

writes that the ability to change the size of one's bets from one hand to the next is critical to a card counter's success. Unfortunately, this makes him vulnerable to exposure, so prudent counters limit their bet variations... winding up with limited profits.

"Most of the time the casinos act out of ignorance," says card counter Howard Grossman. "Most card counters don't win. Casinos can do what they want, but they shouldn't be allowed to throw you out." It is rather unhospitable, but even the Nevada Gaming Commission has arbitrarily barred card counters from state casinos. This does not seem fair, and one comes away with the feeling that it is all right to play blackjack...just as long as one has not won anything.

Actually, the casinos have their own way of dealing with card counters without resorting to edicts from the gaming commission. Most games are now dealt with plastic shoes that hold up to eight decks of playing cards. Dealers reshuffle after two or three hands if a suspected card counter is present. The Union Plaza, Golden Nugget, and several other casinos are using "automatic" shoes, which randomly reshuffle cards after each hand.

Can a person make a living as a blackjack card counter? Uston did. Grossman says, "You win a certain percentage over a period of time." Gollehon writes, "If you can't keep count and you refuse to learn basic strategy, then blackjack will end up about a 5% game for the house, *or better*!"

According to gaming statistics, blackjack tables at Nevada casinos contributed 23.4 percent of the total casino win in a recent one-year period. That is the largest contribution of any table game or slot denomination, and forecasts for the future are even rosier. So just how badly have all these lowly "dregs-of-society" card counters hurt Las Vegas? William Shakespeare said it best, "Methinks thou does protesteth too much." After which he is believed to have said, "Filleth my goblet one mo' time!"

Legendary showman P. T. Barnum made his fortune extolling midgets, sword swallowers, bearded ladies, fat people, skinny people, tattooed people, and others with such hideous abnormalities as an extra leg or an attached twin brother. It was gruesome fare at best, but the public loved it. Barnum's secret was in his famous quote that a sucker was born every minute. . . and nowadays when these unwitting souls are not buying used cars or answering chain letters, they are usually browsing through the personals in the morning newspaper.

This ad recently appeared in a Las Vegas daily. The phone number has been blacked out in order to spare the unsuspecting.

$250,000
PROFIT
Per Year Playing Craps

Let a long time Las Vegas professional gambler teach you with personal instruction, written material and casino play.

UNCONDITIONALLY
GUARANTEED

to be the only approach to win at craps in the long run. Cost is $500, or $300 down and 50% of your winnings when I'm with you. All fees REFUNDABLE if you don't learn & win.

Call ▮▮▮▮▮▮

If a professional gambler had indeed come up with such a winning formula, would it make any sense to share his pot of gold with the rest of the world? Consider the true story of the former casino worker with a similar system of his own. After untold hours of study and research, he began to bet a certain way on the "Don't Pass" line at the craps table... which meant that when the house won *he* won. Almost. In a year's time, he amassed $40,000 with his strategy. The following year he lost all of it, and is still betting the same way — using social security checks as his last bit of collateral. He is easy to spot at the table. He always has the same clothes on, and the same pained expression on his face.

Another thing to avoid is "sports investment consultants," or professional touts. These human piranha charge around $150 for routine predictions, but charge extra for last-minute phone selections that can up the cost to $2,000 or more!

A common scam among dishonest sports services, as they are also known, involves a "Money back if you lose" or "Pay only if you win" guarantee in their advertisements. In fact, the ad we just printed about the craps system is strikingly similar. Note the words, "All fees REFUNDABLE if you don't learn and win."

Think about it. The promoter of these foolish ads is in a rosy position. If you win, he "earns" his fee. If you lose, it doesn't cost him a cent. But it costs *you*! He certainly isn't going to cover your losses for you! The sports service has a nearly 50% chance of winning its fee. It would be like playing blackjack in a casino where if your hand wins, you win the bet; but if the hand loses, you get your bet back. Such a deal!

In yet another scam, a crooked sports handicapper will

ask for a large fee on a "lock" game. He tells half of his clients to take a certain side, and tells the other half of his customers to take the *other* side. After the game, he's got half of his customers thinking he's the greatest thing since canned beer, and they're ready to be pumped for even more money. Playing the same game again — quoting one team to half of his remaining customers, and the other team to the other half — he's now got 25% of his original customers who think he's two for two. They send him everything but the deed to their house.

Nevada Gaming Control Board member Mike Rumbolz says he would like to see sports services all closed up. "If they're located in Nevada, they give state gaming a black eye." Some of them claim to pick winners 90 percent of the time, while sports handicapping experts say that picking 60 percent winners for an entire season is exceptional.

Consultants are not to be confused with professional linemakers at Las Vegas sports books. Better known as "oddsmakers," they are paid advisors who establish the point spreads on various games, which are then posted for Nevada's 40 full-service sports books. The opening line will come out around 8 a.m. and appear on practically every sports page in the country.

Sure, sports betting is against the law everywhere except Nevada, but many Americans do not simply accept it — they demand it! Figures on illegal betting vary according to who does the survey, but it is anywhere from 70 to 100 billion dollars a year! Legally, Nevada sports books handle almost a billion dollars yearly, which is a far cry from the $5 million annual turnover of 15 years ago.

For many people, the craving to gamble at sports is almost as inherent as the instinct of self-preservation. It's like getting out on the playing field one more time, but instead of risking a pulled hamstring all one might suffer is the loss of a day's pay and maybe a bruised ego. Sports commentator Heywood Hale Broun put it this way: "It is so universal and its practice is so pleasurable that I assume it must be evil."

A Montana high school basketball player made a free throw in a game one time, only to hear fans from the rival school cheer for him. Why? Because they needed the point to cover the spread. New York City Mayor Ed Koch was once quizzed about the Giants' chances of winning the Super Bowl. His answer: "They will win by more than the point spread, and the spread is now nine and a half points..."

Of course, not every type of wager is permitted, even in Las Vegas. There was the time that evangelist Oral Roberts claimed to have spoken with God. That is admirable, and many of us have done it from time to time. In this instance, however, God talked to Oral. According to the preacher, he was "being called home" if he did not raise $4.5 million for his university in three months' time. Little Caesars Sports Book set the odds on Roberts' departure to the pearly's at 11 to 10.

Rhode Island was a 2,000 to 1 longshot when odds were posted on where pieces of Skylab would fall. J.R.'s sister-in-law was a 7 to 2 pick when Mister Ewing got air-conditioned. Other oddball bets have included: who the winners would be among Oscar nominees, whether the baby of prospective parents would be a boy or a girl, and who — if anybody — was buried inside Lee Oswald's grave. Finally, the gaming board said "Enough is enough already," and everybody got their money back. By the way, it *was* Oswald.

Television is partly to blame for all the zeal and all the

appeal of sports betting today. Frontier Sports Book Host Lee Pete says, "It's great. You can sit there and watch your money dribble away. But you can't stop it, gambling is something that's inside every man. They had gambling during the Crusades, you know. When Richard the Lionhearted left London, they made him 7 to 2 not to come back. And a lot of people took it."

Pete does a daily radio show in Las Vegas, offering his picks of the week laced with humor. "I ran the bus to Boulder Dam for two years," he says. "I left every Tuesday at 9 a.m. It was a suicide bus for people who bet Sunday and Monday night football. I charged $100, but I gave them a box lunch, and the nicest part of the whole thing was I did a video tape of every guy before he jumped...for his family."

Pete says he has not gambled himself since 1945. "I married a Jewish girl, and that cured me." Horse racing? "It's the sport of kings, but remember, kings never worked." Keno? "In case of an earthquake, go to a Keno lounge. To my knowledge, nothing has ever been hit in one."

In a more serious vein, Pete says, "When you're betting sports fulltime, you have to fight one thing: breakage. Every time you bet a thousand dollars on a game, you have to throw $100 in the kitty. You're talking eleven to ten, and it's very, very strong." That 11 to 10 edge is the vigorish, the commission charged by the sports book on each transaction. The book also has to pay a federal excise tax, which at one time was so high it almost killed the industry.

Sonny Reizner, Executive Director of Sports Gaming at the Frontier Hotel: "When I first came to Vegas in 1970, there was a ten percent federal excise tax. The customer had to lay 110 to 100 for the privilege of his choice, and then he had to give eleven more dollars to the federal government. So actually, the customer was betting $121 to win 89 bucks.''

Small wonder that there were only six sports books in the whole state. U.S. Senator Howard Cannon fought to get that tax lowered, and in 1975 another law was rescinded which had prohibited state casinos from having sports books inside the hotels. ''Frank Rosenthal of the Stardust put in the first hotel sports book that year,'' Reizner remembers, ''and that was followed by Johnny Quinn at the Union Plaza downtown. It was a beautiful opera house type of sports book.''

Yesteryear's smoke-filled, tile floored books are virtually gone. In their place are the sleek, sassy, computerized arenas that abound today. Sports fans love them, if construction figures are any indication. The Las Vegas Hilton spent $17 million on its Superbook which boasts 46 video screens; 30,500 feet of space; and even a $150,000 statue of the racing horse ''Man O' War.'' Caesars Palace doled out $20 million a couple of years back just to make its sports book bigger. Some believe that the Vegas of the future will be nothing *but* sports books — and slot machines. Reizner says, ''When I first started, people would ask me which casino had a sports book. Now they're better off asking which casino *hasn't* got one. The few places that don't have them will have them soon. You can count on it.''

The latest craze at several Las Vegas sports books requires a minimum entry fee, with prizes that stagger the imagination. We're talking TV sets, VCRs, Corvettes, pickup trucks, ski boats, weekly cash prizes, and even a $100,000 four-bedroom home!

One such event comes off every September at Palace

Station, a mile off the dazzling Vegas Strip. The "Great Giveaway" football contest attracts some 16,000 entrants at $25 a pop. What makes this tournament so different is that not only do the contestants with the best records win prizes, but also the ones with the worst records.

Bobby Lancaster won a 1,980 square-foot home, after picking 157 losers in 212 games. The retired bartender found out, though, that nothing in life is really free — not even in Las Vegas. "I don't think I can afford a place like this," he said. The federal tax on the house was $35,000.

The contest sounds like a dream come true, but the drawback is that each contestant must go *inside* Palace Station to make his weekly bets. . . past the gaming tables, the restaurants, the bars, the slot machines. Palace Station is giving away some nice stuff, granted, but Palace Station is also getting 16,000 people a week tripping over one another.

Sports host Lee Pete believes contests like this will hurt Las Vegas in the long run. "This is the greed of the hotels trying to get more people into their places. Take a guy who's going to bet $2,000 in pro football. Now, instead of that, he goes to a couple of hotels and gets in these contests. He's got all the agony he needs for the whole year. I think it's going to dry up a lot of players who used to come out here and spend a lot of money. It's probably going to save a lot of marriages, though."

We asked Pete if a person could make a living betting sports. "I would say five percent can make a go of it, if you adhere to a lot of rules. First, you must start with a bankroll. You can't just play out of your pocket.

"A friend of mine likes basketball. When the NBA season starts, he puts $50,000 aside. Now, he will never bet more than eight percent of that bankroll on any one game.

That way, he is only betting more when he is winning, since the bankroll goes up every time he wins a game. But as he loses, the eight percent becomes less out of the bankroll.''

Pete said that most gamblers bet with their hearts. ''Those guys generally end up wearing Nikes with the toes out of them. Every successful gambler I know has iron-clad rules. A good player never likes to overlap one sport into another. And that old expression — 'Gee, there's a game on television, I'll bet a dime on it' — absolute suicide.''

Sonny Reizner does not gamble now, but remembers those other times clearly. Speaking from his hole-in-the-wall office at the Frontier, he recalled blowing a nine dollar unemployment check on the lowly Boston Braves in 1937. It was the first bet he ever made. ''And there's no telling how many millions of dollars I turned over since then,'' he added. ''Winning it, losing it, betting it, having it, not having it. But I managed to survive. I lasted. Very few people do.''

Could a person make a living betting sports? ''If you have good handicapping ability, discipline, money management, a lot of courage, are ready to sacrifice family and social life, if you know your stuff and you're not afraid of good hard work... gambling can be beaten. But it's not easy.''

Reizner made it all sound so — dismal. ''When you bet sports, there are terrific highs and lows,'' he went on. ''I mean, you hit the nadir of despair...so low you feel like dying.'' His face brightened then, but the somberness of his words echoed in the tiny room. The pictures on the wall of Jim Brown, Ted Williams, Joey Maxim, Jim Plunkett had suddenly lost a little something.

Perhaps Sonny thought so too, for he broke into a smile,

and you could tell a story was coming. "I used to go to Miami every year," he started. "There was a lot of gambling there at the time, so every year I'd meet these fellows in Miami and we'd do our betting. The night before I was supposed to leave, I lost $25,000 on some pro basketball games. So I didn't even go.

"About a week later, one of the guys called me. 'Sonny, where were you? We waited all week for you.' I said, 'I didn't feel like going, I lost a ton of money.' 'You were lucky,' he said, 'it rained all week.' "

Reizner was on a roll. "Another time I went to Miami with a friend of mine, and we won a sizeable amount of money shooting craps. Afterwards we said goodnight and went to bed. The next morning I went to meet him for breakfast, and the guy seemed sad. I asked him what was wrong, and he said, 'I couldn't sleep last night. I tossed and turned with all that money under my pillow, so I grabbed the money, went out and shot craps, lost it and slept like a baby.' "

After talking with Sonny, and Lee Pete. . .after nearly getting an ear gnawed off listening to Pug and the Grand Old Man and all the others. . .one thing became obvious. A person could do it — if he played his cards right. He could make a living as a professional gambler. It was nearly a 25 to 1 long shot, and it called for more sacrifices than most of us would care to make, but it was possible.

Somehow, though, a regular job did not seem so bad after all.

CHAPTER 8

Last of a Breed

Benny Binion is the sole owner and proprietor of Binion's Horseshoe Hotel and Casino in downtown Las Vegas. His club sits smack in the middle of Glitter Gulch, like the foreman's house on a cattle ranch. On the street it was a sleepy Autumn afternoon, but inside Binion's you needed a traffic light to make a left-hand turn. Nine dice games were cranking, and 34 blackjack tables were full of elbows and beer bottles.

I was a little tentative as I inched my way past the big mahogany bar and down the stairs to the steak house. I was here to interview the legendary Benny Binion himself, and it gave me the same kind of feelings Number Six must have had when he went up against Billy The Kid.

I had always liked the man, partly I guess because of the name. Benny Binion. It was like the handle of a schoolmate, of a pal. I would not have liked him as much, I don't think, if his name had been - say - Benjamin Binion. Something else I liked about him was the homespun way he threw his words together. For instance, I had read somewhere that Binion attributed his so-called foresight to "grift." He explained that this meant "sense, knowing how to git along. We was all grifters in those days. All we had was grift sense. There's more grifters in Las Vegas than anywhere else. I'm still a grifter." (I later looked the word up in Webster's, which defined it as "living by one's wits.")

An interview with Benny Binion was important, because his was the only pure gambling joint left in Las Vegas. The corporations that began slithering into town in the late '60s and early '70s had practically made casinos like the Horseshoe an endangered species, so it was not an exaggeration to say that Binion was the last of a dying breed.

His life read like an old James Cagney movie. That morning I had spread out a pasture full of yellowed newspaper clippings, and gone through them like old stamps. He had "grifted" his way from poverty to sainthood, and now he was an old man in poor health. Somehow it didn't seem fair.

I was at the entrance of the restaurant by now, where a small glass case rested next to the wall. Inside it were small waxen figures of Binion and his wife, she simple and plain in a gingham dress and he wearing his famous mammouth buffalo coat...and you could almost hear them saying, "Welcome home." Through the doorway sat Benny himself, holding court at a round table toward the back of the room. I recognized his son Jack, and former federal judge Harry Claiborne. The others were nondescript, reminding me of a sheriff's posse for some reason.

The waitress cleared a table, right next to the big one, and while I waited for Binion to join me I browsed through the menu. The prices were dirt cheap by Las Vegas standards. Chili with beans was $1.75, pure chili was fifty cents extra. There were things on the menu like chicken fried steak, fried catfish, baby back ribs, none of them higher than $4.95. With Binion sitting less than five feet away,

it was like being inside his own personal dining room —
on a ranch somewhere back in time.

Suddenly he plopped down alongside me, with no fanfare at all. Just a little grunt, and there he was. He was
smaller than I thought he would be, and if asked what I
noticed first I would have to admit it was the stubbly
whiskers on his face. He looked like he had been riding
herd for two or three days, but on him it was just natural.
He had the brawny hands of a roustabout, and he was
decked out in ostrich leather cowboy boots and a silk
cowboy shirt with about two dozen gold-plated buttons
on it.

"Git yourself somethin' to eat," were his first words.
I wanted to pepper him with a dozen questions at once,
but he never gave me the chance. "See that gal over
there?" he grumbled, gesturing with a nod of his head to
a table across the room. "I knowed her ever since she was
three years old. She's a mull-tie millionaire. That ole gal
is as sharp as a goddamn tack. She'll put a snake in your
pocket and ask you fer a match." In a louder voice he
called over to her. "Yall come down here fer supper and
I'll visit with yuh." The woman smiled back, and with all
her money she still looked grateful.

"Yawta try the chili," he said, squinting at me through
eyes that had seen eight decades of western sunsets. I gave
the waitress a nod. Her name-tag read "Mother," which
seemed proper enough under the circumstances. I complimented Binion on his Horseshoe Club right off the bat,
because - damn - I felt right at home all of a sudden.

"I could've had a whole lot better if I'd wanted," he
answered, waving at somebody else across the room. Then
he looked back at me, and added, "I always rather take
my chances ownin' a place like this than one of them big

hotels and owe money.''

I had noticed that the Horseshoe did not have a show-room of any kind, not even a lounge for that matter, and I asked him about it.

''The reason I never went fer the shows, I don't know nothin' about it. If you don't know anythin' about talent, you got to hire some sucker that you don't know nothin' about. And then if he gits you a bad one fer two weeks or a month, you're dead. I like the shows, and they're necessary, but I don't need 'em.''

I asked him to describe the Horseshoe Club in his own words, and he took his time answering.

''Well, it's got to be a friendly place. Treat people with courtesy, feed 'em good. Cheap. Good whiskey cheap. And give 'em a good gamble. That's all there is to it, son.''

I questioned him about his early years, although I knew most of it by heart.

''My dad was a livestock trader and a gambler,'' he answered. ''We lived on a farm that belonged to my grand-father when we was broke, which was most of the time. I'll tell you what, you heard about bein' born rich? I was born rich in nineteen-four and in nineteen-eight I come near starvin' to death. There come a big drought over a wide area, a money panic is what it was. And they lost ever-thin' they had. I just hustled, never did work. They had what they call a 'trade day' in ever town then. Be on the first Monday, the second Monday, or this that and the other. I'd make the rounds..gamble..play cards.''

He excused himself to take a phone call and I lit into the chili. It was good all right. But I knew one thing. I did not want to waste any more questions talking about Benny Binion's early years, because I had all of that in my files. Still, it was a helluva story, and I reviewed it in my head as I ate.

He could say he never worked, but on paper the story was a whole lot different. Instead of going to school like other youngsters, Benny was leading mules at county fairs for horsetraders — horsetraders who gambled. While other kids were studying algebra and English, Benny was learning what beat what in seven-card stud. Later he got a job parking cars for gamblers at Warren Diamond's place in Dallas. This opened no doors for him, but it cracked them a little, and young Benny saw a world he would never forget.

It was a wild and wooly time in the nation's existence. Prohibition was starting, a Depression was coming. Like Binion himself was fond of saying, though: "Tough times make tough people." So he went into business for himself, carving a niche as a bootlegger. Seven year Scotch became seven day Scotch, and it was still seven dollars a bottle. Then some dirty lowdown varmint got heavy-handed with Benny's illegal intoxicants, which resulted in said varmint getting ace-deuced and Binion getting a suspended sentence. Asked about it later, Binion would only say, "Well, we had a gunfight and he lost."

About this time, Benny started gambling fulltime. Slowly he accumulated the savvy and know-how that would fill his saddle bags later on. For awhile he ran his own dice game in Texas, with a dizzying limit of $8,000. This was during the days when Las Vegas clubs would only fade $200 on the tables. "No matter what the law said, gamblin' in Texas was just as popular, if not more so, than rodeos," he once reflected. Who cared if it was illegal? It was fun, and for Benny it was profitable.

By the time World War II ended, Binion had become "kind of the boss of gambling down there in Dallas," his son Jack later said. Two years passed, and in 1947 Binion headed west, arriving in Las Vegas with a trunkful of $100 bills and a hankering to run a legitimate casino. The town's population was around 18,000 at the time, and the Strip was nothing more than a wide spot on Highway 91. When asked later if he had any idea of how Las Vegas would grow and prosper in the frantic years to follow, he would say, "Hell no. If I knowed that I would've had it all."

Binion got the feel of the place by going to work at the old Las Vegas Club, right down the block and in the shadows of a spanking new symbol for Las Vegas — the friendly "Howdy Pardner" cowboy known as Vegas Vic. He turned down a chance to buy a place on the Strip, where only three hotels were open, and rejected a $3 million offer for the Golden Nugget. "Too many hidden strings," he said.

By 1951 Las Vegas was booming. United Airlines was flying into a new little airport called McCarran Field. The University of Nevada, Las Vegas, was holding night classes at the local high school. Movie star Jane Russell was in town to make a movie called "The Las Vegas Story," and a cowboy named Benny Binion opened a joint called The Horseshoe Club.

"I had the first carpet on the floor downtown," he once recalled proudly. Craps was the big game at the Horseshoe, and no one played blackjack the way they do now. Slot machines? That was sissy stuff. "I had about a hundred," he recalled one time, "which I gave to this fella who worked fer me. He was a thief, and I figured he was gonna try and steal 'em anyway." The hotel side of the business never interested him, and to this day the Horseshoe has but 80 guest rooms. "Never saw no sense spendin' a lot of money on things I didn't understand."

Binion dropped back into his chair just as I pushed the

empty bowl away. I had heard that he tasted the chili every day, and I mentioned it to him. He shook his head. "I can look at food and tell if it's cooked right. Never cooked a thing in my life, but I been runnin' these joints fer 60 years and always had a kitchen. Even when you violated the law, you had a kitchen."

It made sense to me. He just stuck to the basics, and everything else fell into place. His rule in gambling, for instance, had always been that a man ought to be allowed to bet as much money as he came walking in with. "That's the ole time way of doin' it," he once said. "Players never gave me no trouble. I treat 'em nice and fairly. I never said a cross word to a player. The only people I don't like is the ones that try to snatch my money away. There's always been troublemakers. Everythin' ain't perfect."

Our conversation turned to an incident that had stuck in his mind for half a century. It happened when he worked for Warren Diamond, and he told me about it now. "Ole man Buck Hanlon come in one day. He was one of the richest men in Texas then. He had this brown envelope in his hand he throwed into the dice game. He said, 'Diamond, I want to make your luck.' Diamond said, 'Shoot the dice.' He caught a point and then he lost it. Opened the envelope and it had 170 one-thousand dollar bills in it. And that was back in the days when a thousand dollars was real money.

"I'll tell you one thing about us," Binion continued, propping his elbows on the table. "We have never wrote a man a letter about what he owed, or said a cross word to him. It was our fault when he got it, we didn't have to give it to him. I've wrote off guys that'd come and pay it, and wouldn't stand to be wrote off. 'You can't write me off,' they'd say.

"And I'll tell you the funniest thing that ever happened.

There was a guy, a well-known person, but he kind of got whacky a little bit. Well, he gave us some hot checks a long time ago. I took 'em just to let him play, cause he'd lost a lot of money. Then he come in here a while back and he had a roll of bills this big around. So he ordered a cup of coffee and give the guy a twenty dollar bill. And he's watchin' me to see if I was lookin' at the money. So he said, 'Benny, you still got those old hot checks I give you?' I says, 'I don't think so.' 'I'm gonna play then,' he said, 'but I didn't want to go up there and win, and then git paid off with them hot son of a bitches.' " Benny let out a whoop that brought the waitress running. "God *damn*, and he WIN!" he hollered, shoveling up chuckles from way down in the mine.

I let him catch his breath, and then he started up again like an old steam engine. "I always gambled to fit my bankroll. If I was to lose the bankroll, I'd go to dealin' twenty-five dollar limit...till I got hold of me some money."

Did he ever have to do that? "Yeah, long time ago. Hell yes."

Of course, times had changed since then. "There was a guy that come into town one time, and he had fifteen million dollars. Name was Murphy. So we was tryin' to git hold of 'em. Jack says, 'What if he wants to bet a million dollars a pop?' I said, 'Well, we'll try 'em a few rolls. We can quit any time we want to.' "

Benny was up on his feet again, dishing out another "howdy" to somebody close by. He gave me a fatherly smile that said he would be back, and left me to stare at my empty chili bowl.

One of the reasons so many people were in the club paying their respects to the old man was because he had just celebrated his 83rd birthday. "Celebrate" was indeed the right word for it, since he'd had three heart attacks already. No one ever asked him how he was, because his standard answer now was, "Breathin's hard, walkin's hard, and I can't do nothin'." It made you want to give him a half a buck for coffee, and here he was one of the richest men in town.

So anyway, Benny had celebrated his 83rd birthday two nights ago at the Thomas and Mack sports arena in Las Vegas. This is a big dome-type building with regular stadium seats, where the UNLV Running Rebels play their home basketball games. It turned out to be the biggest birthday party in the history of Las Vegas. Nineteen thousand people showed up, including Benny's inner circle: ex-Sheriff Ralph Lamb, ex-Mayor Oran Gragson, ex-Federal Judge Harry Claiborne, and ex-casino owner Moe Dalitz.

The party was free, and the only stipulation was that tickets had to be picked up at the Horseshoe Club. There was one announcement made on a local radio station, which resulted in the biggest panic since the run on the banks during the Hoover administration. Nobody expected anything like it, and the party wound up costing the Binion family close to half a million dollars before it was over.

Well-wishers were stacked to the rafters, and down on the floor were row after row of folding stadium seats piled full of more people. Twenty rows back from the stage were two oversized easy chairs. Benny was in one, and Moe Dalitz was in the other. Those seated nearby included Gene Autry, Dale Robertson, and Steve Wynn, along with Lamb, Gragson and Claiborne. A few reporters were milling around, one of whom interviewed Moe Dalitz for quite a few minutes. He kept firing question after question, while Dalitz — who is pushing ninety — merely smiled and

nodded his head in reply. Finally, Binion leaned over and
said to the reporter, "You can talk to 'em all you want to,
son, but he can't hear a damn thing."

Just getting inside turned out to be quite an emotional
experience. Binion's big black limousine was parked next
to the entrance, with HRSHOE 1 on the license plate. That
got the adrenalin pumping. Then too, the National Finals
Rodeo was in town, using a nearby parking lot as a corral
for its horses. Consequently, it all seemed rather fitting.
Here was this old cowboy throwing a birthday party for
"a few good friends," and as the throngs of celebrants
passed by, there came this unmistakable aroma of good
ol' western horse shit.

One possible explanation for the extremely large turn-
out was the fact that there was going to be free beer for
everyone in attendance, free entertainment by Willie
Nelson, Hank Williams Jr., and Eddie Raven, free birthday cake, and more free beer.

Someone pointed out Binion's daughter Becky Behman,
and she told me a little more about her dad while Eddie
Raven got the show underway. "He almost died four years
ago," she said, and then she corrected herself. "He did
die and they brought him back. He was so sick and so fra-
gile, so we had nurses for him around the clock. But he
wouldn't mind them, he wouldn't do anything they said.
This one nurse was really getting nagged. She said to him,
'Look, it's time you and I had a little talk.' He said, 'Okay,
I'll start. You're fired.' "

Her eyes sparkled as she talked, and the love was louder
than the music. "I have a little boy who's autistic, and
Daddy just worships him. He wanted a pig for Christmas,
so Daddy got him a pig. Then he wanted to take the pig
to school, to show to his friends. My son's tutor said to

Daddy, 'Mister Binion, how are we going to get the pig to school?' He said, 'Well, we'll call a limousine fer him.' The other kids were more enthralled with seeing the limousine than they were with the pig.''

She told how her son wanted Benny to take him to the movies. Binion, who had apparently not been to a picture show in many years, called the theater and tried to make reservations. "As a dad, he's the greatest," Becky said. "He once baby sat my kids, and when I came back four days later they were wearing the same clothes as when I left them.''

As soon as Eddie Raven finished his performance, Willie Nelson began his. The entertainers were not just playing a couple of songs. Each was doing a regular one to two hour concert, which gave everyone plenty of time to keep ordering more free beer. Willie finally hit his last twang, just as eleven o'clock began to flirt with midnight.

Binion was then led onstage by Steve Wynn, president of the Golden Nugget. The crowd began to chant, "Benny, Ben-ny, Ben-ny," quieting down long enough for Wynn to say, "We think Benny Binion is one of the greatest guys we ever met, and we hope he's around for 83 more years." Benny took the mike and said, "Thank you fer comin'. I never dreamed it'd be anythin' like this. I'll do it again someday. God bless you all.'' Out came a four-tiered birthday cake followed by the proverbial "Happy Birthday To You," followed by more "Ben-ny, BEN-NY, BEN-NY.''

Then it was time for more music, and now young Hank Williams was going to have his turn. It was immediately obvious that Hank Williams Jr. was not there to pay tribute to anything or anybody. Instead, he had decided — for some strange reason — to do a rock and roll concert. This sent Gene Autry right back to Melody Ranch, with Dale Robertson close behind. Putting up with tom toms was one thing, listening to this racket was enough to make a cowboy cram his stetson clear down past his ear lobes. Eventually even Benny Binion could take it no longer. About the only member of the entourage who still seemed to be enjoying the show was Moe Dalitz, who kept smiling and nodding his head.

The mood of the crowd, though, was starting to change. Some of the people down below, mostly the ones wearing furs and diamonds, were leaving their seats in droves... which resulted in a mad dash by the Levi crowd for choicer accommodations. Not only that, but the beer was starting to run low, and now an occasional fist fight was breaking out. This brought in the local militia, while Hank Williams Jr. continued to bombast the remaining survivors with "a wop bop a loo bop a lop bam boom."

The whole evening was full of little ironies. What more fitting end to a memorable event such as this, than a God fearin' hard drivin' beer drinkin' gut bustin' free for all! Then there was the ceremony of Steve Wynn introducing the Horseshoe patriarch. It almost symbolized a royal coronation — the old king making way for the young prince — the end of one era, the beginning of another.

Now, here sat Benny Binion in his premier pleasure palace, doing what he'd done all his life, surrounded by a devoted family that included two daughters, two sons, seven grandkids, and four great-grandchildren. The accolades from all his friends were still fresh in the morning papers. "He's a champion," downtown casino owner Jackie Gaughan said. "He's one of the greatest guys in Las Vegas."

"He's the funniest man there is," said Harry Claiborne.

"There's not an ounce of deceit in him." An unnamed competitor called him an original, and added, "No one has ever been able to imitate him."

Who else would put a million dollars in cash right in the middle of his casino? Benny Binion did. "I got the idea visitin' Washington D.C. There was this long line of people waitin' to visit the U.S. Mint, just to look at money. Seemed to me that it would be a good investment to put a million dollars on display in our casino, just fer the heck of it. You'd be surprised how many people come by just to have their pictures taken standin' alongside all that money."

This brought to mind the funny story of the time several years ago when the money, all in $10,000 bills, had to be temporarily moved to a local bank. "We had new guards at the time, so I gave the boys a money box and sent 'em over to the bank tellin' 'em I'd be along in a few minutes. They opened the box when I arrived, and everone's jaws dropped a foot cause it was filled with cut-up paper. I was carryin' the million dollars in my western boot."

Benny joined me at the table once again, offering no apologies. None was needed. I could see the fire starting to fade in his eyes, and other questions would have to come fast. Cautiously I brought up the subject of the corporations now riding herd on the town, wondering out loud if this was really good for Las Vegas.

"Well, good a lot of ways, bad a lot of ways," he replied. "See, they don't give up nothin' to the politicians, leave 'em all on us. I'll tell you what, I don't doubt that what they're not really good fer us. But if a town's gonna be this big, it has to have 'em. Just like when Hughes come in here. People didn't like it, but people he bought out they took the money and bought other stuff. And things got to rollin' pretty good around here.''

He jabbed a thumb toward the wall behind him. ''Now that Steve Wynn over there at the Golden Nugget, he's done an awful lot fer downtown...I knowed Steve ever since he come here in the whiskey business. Then when he got that thing over there he didn't know what to do with it. We told 'em how to do everthin' but he didn't copy us over there. He copied everthin' we do in Atlantic City, and then he sold out. When he opened up in Atlantic City he said, 'This is gonna be a Binion outfit.' One thing about that son of a bitch, he's sharp.'' Binion chuckled, lapsed into silence while he thought things out, and then spoke again in a scratchy voice.

''I'll tell you who I look up to. A guy who holds his popularity fer forty, fifty years. He had to do kind of right or he couldn't have done it at all. Gene Autry. He was the first cowboy to sing a song on the radio in New York. He sit out there the other night and he told me we'd been friends 45 years. Jack Dempsey. Ole Nick the Greek. He was a smart son of a bitch. He was a philo-soph-er, or whatever you call it.''

His blue eyes seemed to shine brighter for a moment, like embers in a campfire, as he recollected another tidbit from the past. ''I had me a little ole dice machine one time, used little pee-wee dice. Some guy switched 'em on me. Broke me. Well, this friend of mine was a dice maker. He knowed how to make all kinds of dice, loads and everthin', so I went and showed 'em to him. He checked the dice and he knowed what they did, so he give me some more dice. They come in there the next night and I broke 'em. They never did come back again. I won my money and all they had.''

He took a pull from a small bottle of mineral water. Then, as though he owed the world an explanation, he said, "I never did plan nothin'. I just let it come."

You got the feeling listening to Benny talk that some of the recent changes in Las Vegas were not entirely to his liking. "Las Vegas is losin' touch as a gamblin' town. Losin' touch. There was more pleasure in ownin' a casino in the old days. Everbody who was anybody would see each other everday. We'd git together and play poker or shoot craps in the afternoon. Everthin' was personal."

Binion's favorite game was always craps, and slot machines were still nothing more than a nuisance. "I don't believe that they'll ever come out with a machine that'll take the place of dice. Dice is a physical thing." Even the current trend toward sports books did not seem to faze him. "We're really not money hungry," he grumbled. "We don't want everthin'. We don't want anythin' that aggravates you in any way." He gave me a long stare, as though he were sizing up a pack mule, and then let me peek inside his head for just a second. "You shouldn't allow yourself to git fretted over nothin'. Don't let nothin' bother you that you can't help or control. Now if you did somethin' dumb, that might give you somethin' to worry about."

The old man was beginning to get fidgety now, and it was time to say goodbye. No longer did I find it hard to believe that Benny Binion had molded an empire without a day of schooling. He did it with common sense, his own wad of money, and something called "grift." Now, per square foot of gambling space, he had what was probably the most profitable casino in the world. The last thing he told me, though, was not about money or cards or such.

"I'm most proud," he said, "of holdin' my family together. I'd like to be remembered fer bein' solid to my family, and my friends."

There ain't no better tribute than that.

CHAPTER 9

From Reno With Love

The voice of the stewardess crackled over the plane's loudspeaker. I listened with some degree of uneasiness as she explained how my seat cushion could be converted into a flotation device. This made little sense, since we were flying from Las Vegas to Reno across 450 miles of nothing but desert and mountain ranges.

There were two ways to make the trip. One was a nine-hour ordeal by automobile, past such scenic wonders as the Indian Springs gunnery range and the Nevada Test Site. The second — and most popular method of transport — was a bumpy 55-minute plane ride. I was hoping I made the right decision as I buckled the seat belt on my "flotation device." At least, I was in good company. U.S. Senator Chic Hecht was aboard the same plane, as was Nevada Governor Richard Bryan . . . which gives you an idea as to how small Nevada really is.

It was ironic that Hecht and Bryan were flying on the same aircraft, since both were running for Hecht's senate seat. As the plane levelled off at 30,000 feet, I lurched down the narrow aisle. Perhaps they could give me some insight as to why Reno and Las Vegas were so different both in personality and character.

Senator Hecht: "As both cities get bigger, they become more similar. This is primarily due to the influx of people from other states who are moving here because of all that Nevada offers."

(TRANSLATION: "I am running for reelection.")

Governor Bryan: "You have to remember that Reno is much older than Las Vegas. Reno was the dominant city in the state until the mid 1950s. There is much closer contact between the two now, with a lot more interaction, but they will always be different."

(TRANSLATION: "Chic's got the job and I want it.")

Nevada always has marched to a different drummer. It is the seventh largest state in the country, and number 47 in terms of population. Four out of every five residents live in either the Reno area or in Las Vegas, and 87 percent of the rest of it is owned by the U.S. government.

Reno was born in 1868, when towns in Nevada were springing up wherever the railroad went. A fellow by the name of Myron Lake had built a wooden bridge across the Truckee River, and was charging travelers 50 cents a head to get to Virginia City some 25 miles away. By the time the Central Pacific got there, Lake owned not only the toll bridge but a trading station, an inn, a mill and practically all of the land in sight.

Lake gave the railroad 80 acres of property. The railroad surveyed it, built a depot and deeded half the property back to him. Presto! Reno! Named in honor of fallen Civil War hero Jesse Reno, who had never even been to Nevada Territory.

A San Francisco newspaper reporter described how it was in Reno that first summer. "There is no such thing as rest here. People rush in Reno. All day the hammer and saw are heard, and all night the fiddles scrape and the glasses clink.''

That is the way it was in 1868. Reno was the great dividing point between California and the rest of the country. Miners stripped the countryside, and gamblers stripped the miners. True, gambling in Nevada had been illegal since 1861, but nobody paid any attention. So in 1879 gambling was reluctantly allowed. "Cancel Nevada's Statehood!" roared the Chicago Tribune. Nevada is a "vicious Babylon," exclaimed the Los Angeles Times. In 1910, gambling was again outlawed in Nevada. Not surprisingly, gambling continued. In 1931, gambling was legalized for the last time, and the glasses began to clink again in Reno.

The city was hailed as "The Biggest Little City in the World," with a 70-foot arch across Virginia Street. Thankfully, the slogan beat out other such suggestions as:

"East or West, Reno Serves Best." "Reno, Pearl of Great Price." "The Best In The West." "The Town Without a Frown." "In Progressive Reno, Loiter, Linger, Locate."

Licensed gambling had always been looked upon as something rich people did in Europe when they were not fighting wars, but the gaming pioneers who came to Reno changed all of that. Raymond ('Pappy') Smith opened Harold's Club in Reno in 1935, and he was just what Reno needed. He dressed his dealers in cowboy clothes, hung wagon wheels over the casino, and put up 2,000 billboards across the country proclaiming "Harold's Club or Bust." Two years later, William Harrah bought his first Reno casino. Before his death in 1978, he would build not only his famous Harrah's Club on Virginia Street, but the elite Harrah's Tahoe at Lake Tahoe.

Somewhere along the way, though, Reno lost its grip as the state's top draw. One oldtimer, who left northern Nevada during its heyday, returned to find a new Reno not entirely to his liking. "I remember when you walked into a place and sat in with the real men. And there were no females friskin' around bars, either. If you wanted a drink, you rubbed elbows with an honest cowpoke. Women ran homes. Now they're into gambling. The last bar is down, I tell you."

So that was the history of Reno.

By now I was in my rental car, and looking down at what was left of the Truckee River. A survey was taken recently among Reno residents, with each being asked to list the area's ten top attractions. The Truckee River came in seventh. Gambling finished eighth. In some areas of the town, gambling is finished — period. I drove aimlessly down Virginia Street, past the closed-up Mapes Hotel and the closed-up Pick Hobson's Riverside. Past the Cal-Neva and Circus Circus, while off in the distance Bally's and the Sands poked out of the haze like huge periscopes. Past Eddie's Fabulous 50's Casino, where Buddy Holly booms over loudspeakers. . . and waitresses scurried around on rollerskates until somebody tipped off the Safety Board. Maybe it all comes down to what a local official once said. "Our product is not Harrah's, or the Sundowner, or Bally's. Our product is Reno."

The town is old, with rickety Victorian houses braced alongside office buildings and bare-branched elms. It was March, and back in Las Vegas the trees were already in bloom. I had to chuckle, thinking that not only was Las Vegas leading the way in tourism now. . .but even the foliage got a head start down south.

I was not on a mission of vengeance, however. Sure, I

was from Las Vegas, and maybe folks here would not cotton to a city slicker nosing around. But I was also a history buff, and about the oldest thing I had ever seen in Las Vegas was a cocktail waitress at the Jolly Trolley.

For instance, I knew that the Pony Express used to come through the Reno area on its way to Sacramento. This was back when Lincoln was president. It cost $5 to mail a half-ounce letter and took ten days. Don't laugh. The way things are going with the U.S. Postal Service, history is apt to repeat itself.

The Reno Convention Authority will give you all kinds of pamphlets about the area, but you can get everything off the inside page of the phone book. "In a circular valley roughly 12 miles in diameter, surrounded by low mountains, the Reno-Sparks area is also known as the Truckee Meadows." (The city of Sparks is four miles east of Reno, which prompted a longtime Vegas resident to remark: "Reno is so close to hell that you can see Sparks.") "The median age in the Reno-Sparks area is 32.4 years." (Well, I didn't want to move there anyway.) "It has a population of 120,700 people." (Judging from what I saw later at the Peppermill Hotel/Casino, that is not entirely accurate. It has a population of 120,700 *women*.)

The Peppermill is Reno's newest casino. It has women waitresses, women parking attendants, women maids, women registration clerks, and women dealers. As a matter of fact, I only saw one man in the whole place — and he was in charge of hiring all the women who worked there! Incidentally, he was under 32.4 years of age, but looked to be about 98.6.

My first interview was with Dan Wade, vice-president in charge of operations at Harrah's. It is the only Four-Star and Four-Diamond property in northern Nevada, and hauls in 30 percent of the Reno gaming market. Wade began his career in Las Vegas, working in casinos while going to UNLV. "I got a glimpse of my first teaching contract after finishing school, and it was for $7300. What was bad about that was that I was making $21,000 dealing part-time. I opted to go into gaming."

Wade admits that Reno and Las Vegas clash. "But I don't think you'd want that common entity between the two. We would like to be considered different than Las Vegas...and that's fair. We're two different worlds.

"I had a Vegasite attitude at first," he went on. "I thought that Vegas had it all, that Reno was a kind of mom and pop type store. But when you come into this market, you find that the people here are very genuine. At Harrah's, I have never seen such an attitude as the employees have, or even Reno for that matter. It is a very friendly environment." As an example, he cited the games themselves. "You sit down at a 21 table or play keno, and then go back to Las Vegas and play. See if there's a difference."

Reno currently attracts 6 million tourists a year, and gambling income has flattened out to about $700 million. Consequently, no new resorts are being built there. "We're at our capacity right now," Wade says, "but Reno is on a rebound. I think the seed has been planted for a new opportunity." In Las Vegas, those seeds have already sprouted. Tourism in Clark County peaked at 16 million in 1987, and gambling income was a record-breaking $2.7 billion. Still, to be fair to Reno, its neighboring communities should be included in any statistical comparisons. When Lake Tahoe, Sparks and Carson City are taken into consideration, the figures change dramatically. Close to 12 million tourists visited the area in 1987, and gaming revenues topped $1 billion.

In the last three years, more than 100 companies have moved to Reno. They include Porsche, J.C. Penney, General Motors, Sherwin-Williams, Chevron and Champion Spark Plug. Best of all, these companies are distribution centers. . . not factories. Hence there is no smoke pouring into the atmosphere, and the air stays clean. International Game Technology (IGT), a major slot machine manufacturer, has its main plant in Reno where it spends nearly $7 million a year on research and development — money that stays in northern Nevada. In Las Vegas, 50 percent of the work force is involved in tourism; in Reno only 35% of the people rely on tourists. It all makes for a more diversified economy. Should the day ever come when gambling is once again delegalized, Reno at least could survive.

"Reno has been kept a real nice secret for a long time," Wade explained. "It's been secluded. We're going through some transformations within the city right now, with the streets and beautification projects. And we need to keep doing that." These projects include $45 million worth of improvements to the Truckee River and redevelopment of the 37-block downtown area. Meanwhile, another half a million dollars is being spent in southern California advertising the "New Reno."

"There is still a lot of potential in the northwest," Wade stressed. "Oregon, Washington, San Francisco. We have changed our direction in cultural aptitudes. In the last three years we have picked up on the Asian market. And the Canadian market is a short way from Reno. They love Reno, more so than they do the Southwest."

The reason for that is obvious. The temperature in Reno may wander 50 degrees in either direction in the course of one day, but at least it is tolerable. Las Vegas in the summertime is another story. "We get a lot of Las Vegas customers," Wade said, "but for a different reason. Ours is more for the atmosphere around Reno...the skiing and the clean air, the beautiful surroundings, the fishing, the golfing and Lake Tahoe. Vegas has some of that, but for four or five months of the year it's real difficult to go out fishing on Lake Mead. Unless you do it at night, when it's 94 degrees instead of 115."

Okay, Dan, you made your point. The air is clean in Reno — except when everybody stokes up their wood-burning fireplaces. Then a white cloud hangs over the valley until the wind scoots it off across the Sierras. But the Sierras...ahh, they are something to see.

The majestic Sierra Nevada stands along the edge of this green valley, its peaks dusted with snow. Virginia Street turns into Highway 395, and storied cities are only moments away. Thirty miles south is Carson City, the state capital. Forty-five miles southwest is crystal-clear Lake Tahoe, and two dozen miles to the southeast is old Virginia City. Farms dot the landscape, and horses graze behind whitewashed wooden fences. In the space of a heartbeat, Reno is gone.

I was thinking about Dan Wade's last comments as I took the turnoff to Lake Tahoe. My assumption had always been that in Las Vegas, tourism ruled the economy. In Reno, people seemed to resent the growth that tourism brought. Wade answered by saying, "I don't know why the people here have that attitude, or if they even have an attitude. But I don't think they understand the business workings of Reno, of what makes the city tick. I think we need to go out and explain to our public who's paying the taxes, and who's supporting educational growth, and who's supporting the growth of the town itself — and who isn't."

Reno columnist Dick Odessky knows Nevada better than any other journalist. He was the first gaming columnist in the whole state, and has lived in both Reno and Las Vegas. "We found Las Vegas to be an excellent place to raise our two children," he told me. "And Reno is the same way. You get away from the gaming itself, and these are fairly normal towns. . . progressive but normal."

Then why hasn't Reno used the same kind of aggressive ad campaigns which worked so well for Las Vegas?

"Because too many operators in Reno are still private operators. They have their places paid for, and they just don't really care whether the town grows or not. When Kirk Kerkorian built the MGM Grand in Reno, he set Reno back many, many years. He built the place over the protests of many of his competitors, but he went ahead. This was considered to be the big boom that Reno needed.

"And then it seemed like every other day another casino was being built, because everybody was going to get rich now that Kerkorian had this monster hotel. It was less than a year before these fringe properties started falling by the wayside, and the MGM (now Bally's) has never realized near the potential that anyone had for it. And this has scared a lot of these people. I don't feel that the gambling industry has ever recovered from that."

As for Reno's future, Odessky had this to say. "The 'good old boys' will fight growth to the bitter end. Personally, I think Reno is going to vacillate for another five to ten years, and then I think it's going to grow to what it should be."

Lake Tahoe

My rental car labored up one more grade and then suddenly there was Lake Tahoe. I will not attempt to describe its beauty, leaving that to one who saw it a century before me. From Mark Twain's remembrances in *Roughing It*:

"It was a vast oval, and one would have to use up eighty or a hundred good miles in traveling around it. As it lay there with the shadows of the mountains brilliantly photographed upon its still surface, I thought it must surely be the fairest picture the whole earth affords."

The Washoe Indians found the lake first, but it was "discovered" by explorers Kit Carson and John Fremont. I never was able to understand why when the Indians discovered something, it never counted. Let an explorer discover something, and the whole world went crazy. Christopher Columbus "discovered" America, Hernando de Alarcon "discovered" the Colorado River, Don Juan Cardenas "discovered" the Grand Canyon. Of course, the Indians got even every once in a while. They named a few American states, including one out west that was "discovered" by Hernando Cortez:

Cali (HOT) Fornia (FURNACE)

Tahoe has 72 miles of shoreline, making it the largest alpine lake in the country. At 6,225 feet above sea level, the area gets 450 inches of snow a year, and 300 days of sunshine. If this sounds like an ad for the chamber of commerce, maybe it is. Lake Tahoe has an aura of unspoiled beauty, even with the tangle of fancy resorts here and there.

On the north shore is the Hyatt at Incline Village, formerly known as King's Castle, and there's the famous Ponderosa Ranch where all of the earlier episodes of the top-rated television series were filmed. The aura of Ben Cartright, Hoss, and Little Joe still lingers in this popular tourist attraction. Nearby at Crystal Bay are three casinos: the Crystal Bay Club, the Tahoe Biltmore and the famous old Cal-Neva. Most of the "action," however, seems to be on the south shore. Five casinos practically bump into each other at Stateline — Caesars Tahoe, Del Webb's High Sierra, Harvey's Resort, Harrah's Tahoe, and a yuppie entry called Bill's. Owned by Harrah's, Bill's is designed to capture the younger up-tempo gambler with such offbeat features as dealers in pastel polo-shirts and gaming tables covered in mauve felt. All of that may be well and good, but if they start putting little umbrellas in the martinis, I'm leaving.

Lake Tahoe looks pretty much the same as it did when Mark Twain walked up here from Carson City, and there are 70 reasons why. That is the number of government agencies that hold some degree of authority over the shores of Tahoe. When you talk to the people who work there, you begin to understand why most of them live down in Carson City — or in an apartment so far from Lake Tahoe that it is nothing more than a rumor.

Caesars Tahoe pit supervisor Mike Hoover owned a piece of property in Incline Village, a "planned community" on the north shore. According to the Incline Village Chamber of Commerce, this means "controlled growth coupled with strictly enforced zoning and architectural regulations that ensures the preservation of this exclusive mountain village." Hoover wanted to build a house on his property. Enter the IVGID (the Incline Village Greater Improvement District) and the TRPA (the Tahoe Regional Planning Agency).

"I had to go through 43 steps before I could even get a building permit," Hoover said. "It took me a year and a half to get through those. I had to submit paint chips, rock samples, lumber samples, shingle samples, you name it. Then, when I finally finished all of that, there was a moratorium on building.''

That moratorium applies not only to property owners but to the casino industry as well. Consequently, as Caesars Tahoe pit boss Jim Darrough explained, ''We've got to manage the hell out of these places. The only way we're going to continue to thrive here is through an extremely effective marketing program and through extremely effective management. There will never ever be any more big construction. We only have 446 rooms, and with all our power, influence and money, there is no conceivable way we'll ever be able to have more than we do now. The growth of the Tahoe basin is entirely contingent on legislation through the TRPA — and we're dead. What you see is what you get.''

Few people realize that Lake Tahoe made an important contribution to the early growth of northern Nevada. When the Comstock Lode was discovered in nearby Virginia City in 1859, the miners needed lumber. That lumber, which was used for mine supports and construction, and fuel, came from the woods surrounding Lake Tahoe.

Things got quiet at the lake after the mines played out, and they stayed that way until 1944. That was when Harvey Gross built a small service station — with a few slot machines — against the backdrop of the High Sierras. From these humble beginnings emerged Harvey's Resort, now one of the largest casinos in Tahoe and the only one that is still privately owned. Twelve years later, William Harrah bought the former Stateline Country Club, and by 1958 he had enough property on the south shore to build Harrah's Tahoe.

Five million people a year visit Lake Tahoe, and most

of those people come from California. "We have about $1 million a year to spend in that area," said Harvey's marketing director Roger Derby. "What we have tried to do is stress the difference between this and other resort destinations where people might go to gamble. The businesses here really have to appreciate the fact that we are actually competing with other travel and tour destinations." Indeed, Tahoe is probably the only place in the world that can tell its visitors to go jump in the lake — and get away with it.

Unfortunately, when an area has 17 of the top ski resorts in the country, it also gets a lot of bad weather. This can cause gaming figures to fluctuate wildly from year to year. "It's a difficult market," says Tom Yturbide of Harvey's, "and what makes it so difficult is the great differences between the peaks and the valleys." He is not talking about the scenery, either. In 1983, gaming revenues at Lake Tahoe were $248 million. In 1984, the figure jumped to $285 million. The following year, gaming income went up $1 million, but in 1986 it dropped $5 million. One resort employee said, "The winter weather conditions are so uncertain that after November you might as well just hang a 'closed until spring' sign at the airport."

As Jim Darrough of Caesars Tahoe pointed out, "Nobody drives across six hundred miles of desert to gamble at Lake Tahoe. Our market is 99 percent predicated on people coming up from the (San Francisco) Bay area. I can remember many times when Echo Summit was closed, we were out of work." Echo Summit, at over 7,000 feet, is the only way to enter Tahoe from San Francisco, 225 miles away. "Even as recently as five years ago, there was a major landslide. . .and we had a tremendous slowdown to the point where we had to lay some people off. But for the most part, that has changed.''

How Caesars Tahoe tackled the problem may not work for everyone, but it is a novel approach in this new age. "We buy our business," Darrough said. "We concentrate on the high-end market. We have branch offices all over the world, and we fly these people up here. We roll out the red carpet. Lake Tahoe used to be a very seasonable place. But when South Lake Tahoe incorporated as a city in 1967, it didn't take the city planners very long to figure out that we needed to build this place as a year-around resort...as a destination resort."

Personally, I was impressed. People seemed to have a glow on their faces at Lake Tahoe. I do not know if it was because of the high altitude, or the scenery, or maybe the idea that a sudden avalanche might wipe out the country-side any second. But Mike Hoover at Caesars Tahoe put it best: "The atmosphere is much lighter than it is in Las Vegas. It's a much smaller community, so you don't have the problems you have in Las Vegas. I plan to stay here for the duration. It's a beautiful place, and I think it's going to become a real jewel in the gambling industry."

I climbed into the car and started back down the mountain. A sign off to the right promised "One-Horse Open Sleigh Rides" the next time it snowed. I turned to catch one last glimpse of the lake, and there in the sky was a cluster of tiny twinkling objects. Funny, I had never noticed them in Las Vegas. They were stars.

Virginia City

If it were not for Virginia City, there may never have been a Reno. The only reason Myron Lake got people to cross that bridge of his was because they were either taking supplies into Virginia City — or taking gold and silver out.

At its peak, Virginia City had 30,000 inhabitants. One of the first was a drunk by the name of James "Old Virginny" Fenimore. Legend has it that he dropped a bottle of whiskey — and since he did not want the liquor to be a total waste, he scratched up enough to baptize the town. Old Virginny Town became Virginia City in 1859, and it flourished for nearly 20 years before the mines went sour.

In that short period of time, millions of dollars in gold and silver were wrested from the earth. The riches built steamship lines, palaces, cities, and even helped rebuild a nation after the Civil War. Virginia City was the richest mining town in the world, and it still gets its share of gold. Nowadays, that gold comes from the pockets of 1.5 million tourists a year . . . tourists who go on to Reno and Lake Tahoe. So, in a way, Virginia City is still helping Reno grow.

From a distance, Virginia City probably looks the same as it did a hundred years ago, but up close, the streets are lined with one gift shop after another. Yet, it's a fun town to visit, unlike any other.

Just north of the little town is the old cemetery, where the tragedies of those early days are recorded. One epitaph, in particular, caught my eye:

> "Weep not for me as you pass by
> As you arc now, so once was I
> As I am now, so must you be
> Therefore, prepare to follow me."

Carson City

Carson City is one of the nation's smallest capitals, with a population of 37,000. The town's biggest claim to fame has to be the U.S. Mint that was active there many years ago. Coin collectors know that the "CC" mint-mark on many old coins, especially silver dollars, stood for "Carson

City." Although the mint is now shut down, the building has been turned into a museum of sorts, displaying old things native to the region such as Indian artifacts. So don't bother asking where the Egyptian mummies are.

The town is an all-around wonder. (It's a wonder it is still around at all.) Let me give you the whole history of Carson City. It will not take that long. Besides, I don't want to upstage their museum.

In 1858, two businessmen happened upon this chunk of land in the Eagle Valley. Abe Curry had $500, which was enough to get him into the real estate business. William Ormsby, always the promoter, named the spread Carson City after — you guessed it — Kit Carson. This was to be Carson's reward for discovering Lake Tahoe. Ormsby, meanwhile, ended up with his own bit of glory: his name decorates the Ormsby House in Carson City. And old Abe Curry? Well, with all his money gone, Abe just never had a chance.

Anyway, a year later the Comstock Lode was struck at Virginia City, and Carson City took off like a rocket. The town doubled in size five times in five years, and by the time the silver petered out Carson City was squarely on the map.

But that was a hundred years ago! Sure, all the state offices are still in Carson City, but just try to get hold of somebody. "I'm sorry, he is out of the city today." "Oh yeah? What did he do, go home?" Whenever something important happens, everybody in Las Vegas has to get on an airplane. I mean, it was just like I was telling Governor Bryan on the way over here.

I think columnist Dick Odessky had the right idea. "Perhaps everyone would be better off," he wrote, "if Nevada were split into two states. Or, better yet, perhaps two countries."

It was time. I took one last swing through downtown Reno, and then with the expertise of a cab driver I snagged the on-ramp of the freeway. That was one nice thing about Reno. You didn't have to worry about getting lost.

Critics of the town say it is corny, that it is not in tune with modern society. I found the small-town atmosphere to be part of its charm, and certainly Reno has more historical substance than any other place in Nevada.

Gambling sits on the sidelines in Reno, and always has. First there was "redline" legislation, limiting casinos to a two-block core downtown. That was mercifully changed, but now an ordinance is in effect which closes the door on small operators. No new casino can be built in Reno unless it includes a 300-room hotel. What does that do to people like Pappy Smith and Bill Harrah and Warren Nelson of the Cal-Neva, who made Reno what it is today? Warren Nelson doesn't have *one* hotel room, let alone three hundred.

But I like what Mark Curtis had to say about Reno. He once ran Harrah's publicity department, and currently heads up the Biggest Little City Committee. "For too long we have really been down on ourselves, too critical of our city. Nothing was right. And we would blame anything but the real root of the problem — our own lack of initiative." Now the drive is on "to try to get everybody to recognize the enormous number of assets we possess, which any other city four or five times larger would die for."

By now I was at Reno Cannon International Airport. I stood in line to check in my rental car, stood in line to check in my luggage, and stood in line to get on an airplane. Once again, I listened as the stewardess went through her spiel about flotation devices. . .and bit my tongue to keep from hollering, "Hey, let's talk about *parachutes*!"

The plane rumbled down the runway, full to the brim with people heading south. The stewardess shook her head as she passed by. "Why would anyone want to go to Las Vegas from Reno?" she asked. And for once in my life, I was stuck for an answer.

CHAPTER 10

The Don of Laughlin

Perched on a jutting piece of ground up over the Colorado River was the blue and white helicopter. It resembled some kind of big plastic waterbug, with drooping rotor blades dangerously close to the ground. Walking quite businesslike toward the monstrous machine was a white-haired fellow in a bright red suit that practically screamed for attention. Even bathed in the shadows of the giant Riverside Casino, he stood out like Rudolph's nose on a certain night. As he inspected the helicopter, an old station wagon approached and wheezed to a stop. The door creaked open, and out stepped another man dressed in red. He adjusted his chin whiskers with one hand and his tufted red cap with the other. "Are you Santa Claus?" the white-haired fellow asked. "Yeah," Santa said. Both then climbed into the chopper, a horrible whine ensued, and then they were gone. The pilot was Don Laughlin, flying old Saint Nick to an apartment complex and a waiting crowd of children.

First there was Reno. Then came Las Vegas, and after that Atlantic City. Now it is Laughlin, a brazen little river

156

town that is challenging the big boys and already winning a few hands. Two percent of all Nevada tourists, or one in every 50, have currently been lured to this sun-parched oasis. Gaming revenues there have jumped 60 percent in the last two years, compared with a yawning six percent for the rest of Nevada.

Fifty thousand tourists a week take dusty narrow roads into Laughlin from Arizona and California. Nine casinos rock around the clock, and who knows where it will end. Laughlin is indeed a genuine American boom town, busting at the seams with shiny buildings and high enthusiasm.

Part of its attraction is location, less than a hundred miles south of Las Vegas and right between Phoenix and Los Angeles. The weather is another factor: warm in the winter, warmer in the summer. Sizzling temperatures are no problem, though, since the Colorado River runs right through town. It is a fisherman's utopia, a swimmer's delight, a miner's dream, a gambler's fantasy, and an RV owner's pure paradise.

Laughlin tail-ends off of Davis Dam, which was built in 1953 to control flash floods and generate juice to the area. Coming across the Mohave Desert, past ghost towns and mining camps, almost asleep at the wheel with the boredom of it all, then suddenly up it springs. In the daytime it is like a mirage, at night there is something almost magical about it...thousands of twinkling lights that ricochet off the glassy water, and a line of hotels right out of Miami Beach.

First is the Riverside, owned by town founder Don Laughlin. It has 660 rooms, 1,500 slots, 42 live table games, two movie theaters and the area's only post office.

Next is the Regency Casino, "the smallest but the friendliest," its brochure states. Towering over the Regency is the Edgewater Hotel and Casino, with 37 live games, a 32-lane bowling center and a race and sports book. It is now owned by Circus Circus Enterprises, which has yet to book a loser.

Then comes the Colorado Belle, newest addition to the Laughlin skyline and another holding of Circus Circus. With smoke stacks 21 stories tall, it is a replica of an authentic Mississippi riverboat. The Colorado Belle boasts 60,000 square feet of casino area, as well as five restaurants and 1,238 hotel rooms.

The Pioneer Hotel is next on the five-mile Casino Drive, with 414 rooms, two restaurants and a tennis court. Standing over the river is the Pioneer's mascot, River Rick . . . not to be confused with that other hick named Vegas Vic.

Alongside the Pioneer is the old Del Webb Nevada Club. The Webb Corporation sold it recently to Steve Wynn for $40 million, which breaks down to almost $500,000 a room. The owner of the Golden Nugget says he has big plans for the property, including the construction of a 1,000-room tower.

Up at the top of the bluff is the Sam's Town Gold River Hotel and Gambling Hall. Designed along the lines of an old-time smelting plant, it has 225 rooms and the best 98-cent breakfast in town.

The newest additions to the Laughlin skyline are Harrah's Laughlin Hotel and Casino, and Ramada Station. Harrah's built at a cost of $65 million, is 15 stories high and has a beach right on the Colorado. Ramada Station features the motif of a Victorian railroad station, with a narrow-gauge railway circling the property. It is the only Laughlin casino located away from the river bank, and maybe that is why it only cost $60 million.

Laughlin, which has already overtaken Lake Tahoe as Nevada's number three gambling market, was not even a spot on the map twenty years ago. The dam was there, and the river was there, but the only other thing around was a couple of boarded-up buildings and a lot of peace and quiet. That is when a young Minnesotan named Don Laughlin arrived on the scene.

Laughlin had moved to Las Vegas in 1952. He was destined to become a successful businessman from the start. Born poor, he trapped muskrat and mink, selling the skins and investing the money. He was investing it in slot machines, which he bought from a mail-order catalog. In turn, he leased the machines to nearby taverns, splitting the profits with the owners fifty-fifty. By the time Don was in the ninth grade he was making more than the principal, and that was the end of his formal education. Laughlin headed west, learning two things when he got to Las Vegas — how to deal cards, and how to fly airplanes.

Two years later, he bought a seedy rundown bar in North Las Vegas known as the 101 Club. It had three slot machines and one blackjack table. After eight years he sold it for a hefty profit of $165,000, then began his search for greater fame and fortune. He was 33 years old.

Enter Don Laughlin, pilot. "In flying over the area, I saw Kingman, Arizona, over these hills; Needles, California, down below; and Havasu just beyond. We had 30 or 40 thousand people here, back in the '60s, which seemed like enough to support a casino. The closest competition was Las Vegas."

Laughlin had looked at 25 different locations for his new venture. "This looked like the best," he said. The land he chose was cheap ($235,000 with 15% down), available and right on the banks of the Colorado River. His six acres was at the end of a lonely dirt road and consisted of a bar, a live bait shop and five tumbledown cabins. He had three subordinates, a far cry from the 1,400 people he employs now.

There were no doctors, no hospitals, no police, and frequent power shortages. "We hired the toughest guy around to be the security guard," he remembered. "If he got whipped, we'd hire the guy who whipped him." Laughlin grinned, and then thought back some more.

"When we first opened, we had a lot of amusing things happen. We had wild burros all over the place. They'd come up to the casino windows in the middle of the night, and stick their long faces up against the glass. There'd be two or three of them at the window, staring at you. It was kind of scary, but they were harmless. We had a truck driver who asked to use the phone. We only had one phone at the time, and it was out in the parking lot. So he went out and then came back in all red-faced. 'There's a rattle-snake in the phone booth,' he said. 'Did you kill it?' 'No,' he answered. 'I didn't have to use the phone that bad.' "

Laughlin was unable to finance his operation in the beginning. "Bankers just laughed at me. 'A hundred miles out of town, in the gambling business, and you want to borrow money? We don't have any money.' I listened to that until 1971."

Meanwhile, things were turning sour in Las Vegas. The city had gone on an unprecedented building boom since Laughlin had bought his Shangri-la. New hotels that had sprung up included the Mint, Aladdin, Four Queens, Caesars Palace, International, Circus Circus, Landmark and Union Plaza. Las Vegas was getting fat on tourists and losing its small-town charm.

Laughlin's Riverside Hotel began to get second looks

from people with retirement savings and Social Security checks. Las Vegas was out of their price range, but rooms and meals cost next to nothing at the Riverside. Laughlin bought more land, eventually expanding his hotel property to 92 acres. At the same time he was buying other chunks of real estate, including a 61,000-acre ranch in Arizona's Hualapai Mountains and 520 acres of farmland near Needles.

"My attorney in Las Vegas suggested one day that I put in a post office down here. So we applied, and a guy showed up from the district office in San Francisco. He liked the site and wanted some suggestions as to what to call it. We suggested the names Casino and Riverside. And it came back 'Laughlin.' I didn't see the guy for several months. He came in one day on post office business, and I asked him what made them pick Laughlin. He said they didn't really want to use a casino name, the government doesn't like it. And there's a Riverside in every state and the mail gets all mixed up. 'What the hell,' the guy said, 'Laughlin is a good Irish name.' *His* name, incidentally, was O'Neill."

Now Laughlin had not only his own casino, but in a town *named* after him. He would joke about it in years to come, saying, "No, they named it after my mother."

Retirees and postal inspectors were not the only ones interested in Laughlin. Casino corporations, which had already bagged Las Vegas, decided to put this new town on their trophy wall. Land along the riverfront jumped from $400 a foot to $2 million an acre, or twice the cost of property on the fabled Las Vegas Strip. Circus Circus built two properties, and now operates more than half the market's total room base. Its chairman and chief executive is William G. Bennett. "We get a lot of senior citizens down here now, but in the wintertime, my God, it's strictly senior citizen city. There are a lot of retired senior citizens who've got a few bucks."

As new hotels rose on the sandy shores of the Colorado, the population of Laughlin rocketed from 95 people in 1984 to over 2,500 in three years time. Another 3,000 cross daily from Bullhead City, Arizona, just across the river. Laughlin himself never imagined how rapidly his unincorporated town would grow. "I think we've only scratched the surface. New casinos are opening. The town is getting new housing. We've got shopping centers and there's a lot of construction all over the place. I can see in another 10 to 15 years having 35,000 residents here. People like this area."

Speaking from his wood-paneled conference room overlooking the churning river, Laughlin reflected on his desert paradise. "This area has got more of a personality than a big city. I'm not picking on Las Vegas, but you go to Las Vegas and if you're not acquainted with a hotel you feel like you did something wrong just by coming in. The treatment is terrible, and we hear it all day long.

"The big corporations have made the casinos lose their personality. I think they're easy to compete with because they're not run nearly as efficiently as we can run, and they don't cater to the public."

Laughlin lives right on the hotel property, and thinks of himself as a baby-sitter. "Many times when you're in a big corporation hotel, there's nobody to talk to. I'm always available."

He admits glumly that his enterprises are governed by what his competition does. "We're renting rooms for $18 a night. Circus Circus will rent rooms at any price to keep their place full, so we just fade 'em. If they sell all the food you can eat for three dollars, we sell it for three. We're not going to let them take our business. And that's what they'd do if we didn't follow suit.''

Laughlin, by his own admission, is a millionaire. He dresses the part, acts the part, and talks about huge sums of money in an easy offhanded manner. "I don't mean to slap ourselves on the back, but in the last two years we have donated $17 million. We tell people that what we make here we spend here.'' He paid $6.3 million to the state of Arizona to buy an airport, spent $3.5 million building a bridge connecting Laughlin to Bullhead City, plans to shell out $12 million for flood control and another $4 million for a municipal golf course.

His Riverside Casino has ballooned to 660 rooms, with an additional 385-space RV park just across the narrow street. "Having RVs," he said, "is like having extra hotel rooms. And they are quality people. . .who have raised their families, sold their businesses, and are spending their remaining active years enjoying themselves.'' The people who come to his resort town may dress like cowboys, but many of them are quality tourists who would wear ties and furs anywhere else. That, he said, is what is deceiving about Laughlin's clientele: the "quality" of the people. "We're busy all year long. In the wintertime we get the retirees by the thousands. In the summertime we get the younger crowd with children, who come here for the water sports.''

His casino jumps 24 hours a day, and well it should since it is the first stop on Casino Drive. All those contributions Laughlin made should begin to pay back some beefy dividends. The airport he is building is next to the bridge he built, which goes right up to the Riverside. . .and the proposed golf course he will build is a two-wood from the Riverside's RV park.

The man is successful at what he does, and part of the secret could be the words he lives by. "The harder you work, the luckier you get," he says with a smile. Laughlin had a vision back in the beginning, but he also had the ambition and the fortitude. His energy is still boundless. "I start at about ten o'clock," he recited, drumming his fingers on the table edge. "I'm on the telephone for a couple of hours, getting everybody moving that I want to do certain things. Then I jump in the shower. I get down to the office about two or three o'clock, and then I go to daylight usually. I wouldn't enjoy playing golf or fishing," he added ruefully.

Many of Laughlin's policies have no doubt played a role in his phenomenal success. He allows his dealers to gamble freely at the Riverside. "After all," he will say, "we're running a gambling establishment." In Atlantic City, a professional dealer cannot gamble anywhere in town. In Las Vegas, most dealers are not even allowed to use a public restroom in the hotel where they work. He sells his food so cheaply in his 24-hour restaurant and at his two buffets that he loses $12,000 a day. He justifies it, however, by saying, "If you give the gambler what he wants he's going to come, otherwise he's going to go somewhere else. That's the great thing about America. You've got competition."

He allows tourists to take as many pictures as they want inside the casino. Try doing that in Las Vegas, and you find out in a hurry whether or not your camera is shatterproof.

Laughlin also "four-walls" his showroom. The entertainers are not paid, but instead keep all the receipts from each night's performance. "We get the exposure,"

Laughlin says. "What the stars make is what they make." It works, though, in Don's Celebrity Theatre. Ask Charley Pride, Mel Tillis, Merle Haggard, Sammy Davis Jr.

Down the stairs from the showroom is Laughlin's new "Losers Lounge," where live country music is cranked so loud that patrons order their drinks in sign language. Gallery portraits include Robert E. Lee, Joe McCarthy, George Custer, Nixon and Agnew, and the bar's two favorite modes of transportation: the H.M.S. Titanic and the Hindenburg.

Don Laughlin is outspoken about his casino operation, which is so successful that the Golden Nugget's Steve Wynn once offered him $95 million for it. By his own admission he is worth over $200 million, yet in a quiet moment he thinks of the day when he might just join the RV crowd. Of course, Laughlin — who does everything in a big way these days — would see the whizzing landscape in a Bluebird Wanderlodge, and be driven by his own chauffeur. Bluebirds go for up to a quarter of a million, chauffeurs are a little cheaper.

Laughlin is also outspoken about government red tape and the bureaucratic buzzard known as the I.R.S. "The worst thing that happened to the gambling industry is Regulation 6A," he said, his eyes fierce with indignation. That regulation is a sore spot with everyone in Nevada, which was instituted by the Internal Revenue Service to clamp down on high rollers. Any player whose cash transactions exceed $10,000 in a 24-hour period is reported to the government.

"Our dear friend — the I.R.S. — gets half of what we make, and half of what every other casino in America makes. And then they run a few billion dollars a year out of the country because these people don't want their names turned in to the I.R.S. I don't care if it's the most legitimate guy in the world, he doesn't want his name given to the I.R.S. We've lost hundreds of customers over this damned thing. This is not only hurting us, but the I.R.S. is the big loser. They don't think business, they just think power."

Laughlin was also bristling because his casino had been victim to its first armed robbery the night before. "I couldn't believe it," he said. "A man walked in, stuck a gun in the face of a change girl, and got away with $1,500." Then again, that seems to be one of the sure signs of success these days.

Despite the challenges, the town of Laughlin — like its owner — is on the move. It now has its own elementary school, its own library, and several shopping areas, all of which are less than a year old. The whole area is similar in many ways to the Las Vegas of the early '40s, except in Vegas the waters of Lake Mead are a good hour away. A 14-year resident of Laughlin put it bluntly. "This is going to be one of the biggest recreation areas in Nevada," said Jack Dotson. "We've got the gaming and we've got the water."

"There isn't anything to do here, but it's all coming," another resident said. "It's a pioneer town. I'm here for the growth." Al Cayer, a Laughlin restaurant owner: "It really isn't that convenient to live here. But the population base will come. The potential is super good. I think in a few years, we'll be second in the state only to Las Vegas."

Las Vegas builder Bob Bilbray can certainly attest to the luster of Laughlin. In 1978, he bought 430 prime acres of land there for $2.2 million. "At that time there were only 32 people in Laughlin, none under age 62." Today that land is worth more than $50 million. "There's an incredible potential for commercial development here," he says, "because just about everything so far is a monopoly. But it's moving faster than I ever thought it would."

According to the Clark County Comprehensive Planning Department, only about ten miles in Laughlin have been developed so far. The town, which encompasses a total of 150 square miles, extends to the California border on the south and west. This is the way into Laughlin from California, where 40 percent of the tourists come. A $2.5 million road was recently completed which links the casino area of Laughlin with the Needles Highway. The five-mile extension of Casino Drive makes it easier for motorists to get into town without having to go across the Colorado River into Arizona, then circle back to Laughlin.

Of course, there are still problems to overcome in this Cinderella city. There is the threat of eventual gambling on nearby Indian reservations, which could cut into Laughlin's gaming revenue. There is also the lack of affordable housing in the budding town, and this has become a bone of contention between casino workers and residential developers. As things stand now, most of the work force lives across the bridge in neighboring Bullhead City, where housing is more affordable. The workers must pay an Arizona state income tax, however, and live on a muddled schedule of different time zones. During the winter months, it is six a.m. in Laughlin, Nevada, while less than a mile away it is still five o'clock in Bullhead City, Arizona. It works out all right at night, though, because a dealer can get off work at seven o'clock and still get home in time for the six o'clock news.

Laughlin has casinos, and Laughlin has tourists, but Laughlin does not have: a high school, traffic lights, gas stations, hardware stores, or neat little cafes that give a town its personality. Currently, there are two small grocery stores, a sporting goods outlet, a video rental shop and two banks...one of which is owned by town father Don Laughlin. Nearly all of these businesses, with the exception of the banks, are tucked away from the waterfront in the residential district, excluding them from tourist trade. The residential district should not even be called that, because it is mostly a jumble of sky-high condominiums that are owned primarily by rich retirees and California investors.

Land has to come from somewhere, and in the case of Laughlin most of the acreage is held by the Bureau of Land Management. The government has been selling it off in small lots of five and ten acres, but it is a slow process and forces Laughlin to depend on Bullhead City for services it does not have. That could all change dramatically in the near future. Jim Ley, assistant director of the Clark County Comprehensive Planning Department, says 9,000 acres of land held by the Land Management Bureau is in a transfer area. "In two to three years down the road, the BLM will hopefully be able to consider putting 1,500 to 2,000 acres on the market. And we're hoping it will be sold in large plannable acres."

Two thousand acres of riverfront wilderness near Laughlin have been set aside for a state park someday. Right now there is a compound adjacent to the scrubby land, where a few of the town's residents live. One of them is local fireman Jon Lindbergh. He has seen all kinds of wildlife in the area, including coyotes, foxes, muskrats, beavers, bobcats and rattlesnakes. Lindbergh offered to share his recipe for snake steak. "It's delicious. The meat is white and tastes like chicken."

"Sounds great, Jon."

"It is also stringy like rabbit and oily like duck."

"Gotcha. Thanks, Jon."

"All you do is get yourself a freshly-killed rattler —"

"I'll do it first chance I get, Jon."

"— so fresh the meat still wiggles in the skillet —"

"Well, it was nice talking with you, Jon."

"— and fry it in butter over a mesquite wood fire."

"Gosh, just look at the time."

"Would you like to stay for dinner?"

CHAPTER 11

Away From The Tables

Las Vegas is like a chrome hubcap on an old car. It does not really fit the surroundings, but it looks nice. And if you search a little farther, beyond the casinos, you will find more treasures in this jumbled landscape. There is history here, the winds of the past swooping over ghost towns, mining camps, deserted forts, Indian ruins, wild high-spirited mustangs running free. Even the vast monotony of the great Mohave desert throbs with a heartbeat all its own, and the hushed panorama seems to spill on forever.

The World's Shortest History Lesson

This seemingly barren land coughed up a little water and a few gold nuggets . . . and the Anasazi Indians settled in, followed by the Paiute, the Spanish, the Mexicans, the Mormons . . . followed by the Siegels, the Hughes, the Hiltons, and Ramadas.

Only a few lonely miners lived in Nevada territory during the days of the Civil War. "The nether nook of nothing'' was how the raw countryside was seen by Yankee newspapers. Mark Twain, who worked briefly as a reporter in Carson City, wrote a friend that the town was a den of "booze, wild women and 24-hour gambling. Certainly no place for a good Presbyterian. So I no longer am one.''

In 1864 Nevada became the 36th state of the Union, and by 1909 some 1,800 Mormons were living in Las Vegas, scratching out a thin living from thin ground. Eleven saloons dotted the landscape, and two churches, where funeral services were held for those killed in the eleven saloons. Six years later, Frank Sinatra was born in Hoboken, New Jersey.

Las Vegas was on its way!!

The Strip

The Las Vegas Strip runs from the Hacienda Hotel clear down to the Sahara Hotel, one casino after another. The first resort on the Strip was the El Rancho, where Howard Hughes could be found eating quietly in the Stage Door Steak House. It was built in 1941, ran into financial difficulties in 1959, and burned to the ground in 1960. The big chunk of land, across from the Sahara, is vacant now, but a rumor persists that eventually it will be the site of a Disneyland-type amusement park owned and operated by Circus Circus.

If so, it will fit right in with the new image of Las Vegas, which is geared these days toward the whole family.

Twenty years ago, there was absolutely nothing for a child to do in Vegas except sit in the hotel room and watch "Howdy Doody" on TV. Now Mom can play the slots, dad can shoot craps, and the kids can hang out at the Las Vegas Hilton's Youth Hotel, hit the video arcades at Caesars Palace, Bally's, Riviera and the new El Rancho, or watch continuous circus entertainment at Circus Circus. Funny story: Shecky Greene called Circus Circus shortly after it opened in 1968, asking the owner, "Why did you call your hotel Circus Circus?" Said the owner, "Well, I'll tell you...well, I'll tell you..."

Just south of the Sahara is the sprawling water park called Wet 'n Wild, open each spring and summer. A person not only can bet his life savings in the casino, but also that he will come off the towering Der Stuka water-slide in one piece, which is sometimes all that is left of a girl's two-piece bathing suit. Using a rating system based on the roll of a pair of dice, Wet 'n Wild merits a top roll of:

Kids of all ages can spend the day (and their allowance) at the Scandia Family Fun Center, south of Palace Station off Sirius. There are three elaborate miniature golf courses, an armada of bumper boats, automated baseball pitching machines, and gasoline-powered go carts on the Little Indy Raceway. The park is open year-round.

At the Stardust Hotel, memories merge with modern technology at the Olde-Tyme Gambling Museum, where early gambling equipment is showcased. It costs a dollar to get in, but what's a dollar in Las Vegas? Near the museum, is Ralph's Diner, a hamburger joint right out of the fifties that is sure to tug at the old memory strings. "Maybelline" is on the juke, shrimp baskets are on the menu, and drinks come in those wonderful old-fashioned plastic holders with the little paper cone inserts. Both rate:

Down the Strip is the Imperial Palace Antique and Classic Auto Collection. Located on the fifth floor of the hotel, there are over 200 old cars on display, all in working condition. Among them are Adolf Hitler's 1939

Mercedes Benz, W.C. Fields' V-16 Cadillac, the 1905 Thomas Flyer touring car, and the 1954 Tucker.

At Caesars Palace, there is the futuristic Omnimax Theater housed in a geodesic dome. Viewers sit in fancy reclining chairs and see special movies on a wraparound screen. It is like watching something in 3-D without having to wear those goofy blue and red eyeglasses.

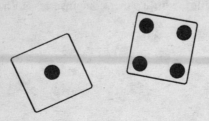

Bally's Theater, at the end of that hotel's shopping arcade, features old classics with a new touch: sofas instead of movie seats, and push-button drink service. Play it again, Sam.

Tyrannosaurus rex and Triceratops share co-billing at the Las Vegas Museum of Natural History, just across the Strip from the Aladdin. Some of the dinosaurs are animated and snap at visitors, especially if they neglect to pay the admission charge.

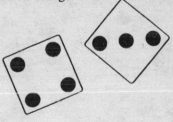

On West Tropicana, off the Strip, is the Liberace Museum. This collection of costumes and props used by "Mr. Showmanship" is well worth the price of admission, which is: "tax-deductible donation accepted." Among the exhibits are the world's largest rhinestone, and pianos once owned by Frederic Chopin and George Gershwin.

Downtown at the Four Queens is Ripley's "Believe It Or Not" Odditorium. There are more than 4,000 items on display in this macabre museum, including a jellybean mosaic that Ronald Reagan would die for. One thing is certain. After encountering all these ingenious and disgusting artifacts, a person will walk out knowing that he's not so weird after all, even though he paid to see this stuff in the first place.

Culture With A Capital "K"

In Lorenzi Park, on West Washington Avenue in Las Vegas, is the Las Vegas Art Museum. Included in the permanent collection of paintings, sculpture and ceramics are new works by Nevada artists. There is a children's museum on the premises, aptly called "Discovery." Kids can push buttons until their fingers go numb, hopefully stimulating their curiosity as they do so.

Also in Lorenzi Park is the Nevada State Museum and Historical Society. The growth of the area from the time of the Spanish explorers is detailed, with another gallery devoted exclusively to the heyday of neon. Admission is free.

There are two museums of natural history in Las Vegas, the one with the dinosaurs and the other at the University of Nevada, Las Vegas. . . better known as UNLV. This on-campus museum features Indian and pre-Columbian arti-facts, as well as an unusual display of southern Nevada greenery, with no greenery required for admittance.

The earliest original building still standing in Nevada is the old Mormon Fort, built by missionaries in 1855. To-day it is a museum off Cashman Field, at Washington Avenue and Las Vegas Boulevard North. The mission was originally situated halfway between Salt Lake City and San Bernardino, California, and was later moved to Las Vegas. Either that, or the San Francisco earthquake was a lot worse that we thought it was.

Driving towards Henderson, Nevada, there is the Clark County Museum off to the left (at 1830 South Boulder Highway). It is actually the old Boulder City railroad depot, refitted to house early Nevada artifacts. Included are mining and ranching tools from the early West, old railroad cars, and even a bungalow from the 1920s.

Another sight worth beholding is one of the largest cac-tus gardens in the United States. It is on part of the Ethel M. Chocolate Factory complex, Sunset Road at Mountain Vista. After seeing the cactus, and enough squirrels to last a lifetime, take a self-guided tour of the candy factory. Nevada and Kentucky are the only two states where boozy

bonbons are made, and they sell for around $10 a bottle
. . .uhh, box.

So much for culture, pass the chocolates!

Sports Shorts

Most Strip hotels have tennis courts, and usually non-
guests can play for a small fee. Among the best are the ones
at the Aladdin, Sands, Las Vegas Hilton, Frontier, Flamingo Hilton, Desert Inn, Bally's, and Caesars Palace
(where Pancho Gonzales is the resident pro). In the summer, plan on playing early in the day or on a lighted court
at night.

Golf is one of the most popular sports in Las Vegas, with
lush greens that loom like mirages in the sand. There are
thirteen courses in the area, including the famous Dunes
Miracle Mile Golf Course. Most of the rest are owned by
other resorts, except for the Las Vegas Municipal Golf
Course, Craig Ranch, the Boulder City Municipal Course,
and the North Las Vegas Community Course. . .a lighted
par-three job.

Raquetball fans can pick from a number of courts, including Caesars Palace, the Las Vegas Sporting House,
and the Las Vegas Athletic Club with three locations.
Bowling is right down your alley at the world-famous
Showboat, with 106 lanes, and at Sam's Town, just outside of town on the Boulder Highway.

Football fans can follow the UNLV Running Rebels at
the Sam Boyd Silver Bowl, while the Thomas & Mack
Center (West Tropicana near Maryland Parkway) is home
to the UNLV basketball team. The farm club of the San
Diego Padres plays its home games at Cashman Field, on

Las Vegas Boulevard North.

In the winter, there is skiing at Lee Canyon, 45 miles west of Las Vegas on the Tonopah Highway. Accommodations include: three double chair lifts for experts, a T-bar for intermediates, and a real bar inside for beginners.

Butting up against Lee Canyon is Mt. Charleston, third highest mountain in the state at an elevation of 12,000 feet. Situated in the heart of the Toiyabe National Forest, the view from the top is glorious . . . glamorous . . . and that old standby, magnificent. Bristlecone pines stand sentry like old warriors, here long before man or any other living thing. There are hiking trails, lookout points, picnic areas, and campsites. There is also the quaint township of Mt. Charleston nearby, and a rustic lodge nestled in the pines up at the end of the road. It's the perfect end ("Two hot buttered rums, please") to a perfect day. ("Watch out for that — boink — tree branch.")

Close Encounters

Red Rock Canyon is an easy 15 miles west of Las Vegas off Charleston Boulevard. A 3,000-foot high mass of pinnacles and boulders makes up Red Rock Escarpment, focal point of this eerie landscape (Take Calico Basin turnoff). Reds and golds blend together in lazy harmony, and a 13-mile scenic loop lets you gawk at Mother Earth without her clothes on.

Two miles down the winding highway is Spring Mountain Ranch State Park. The ranch was the former hideaway of millionaire Vera Krupp, wife of the German industrialist. She sold it to Chester Lauck of radio fame's "Lum And Abner," who sold it to Howard Hughes, who sold it to Fletcher Jones, who sold it to the state parks system. It is well worth seeing, with hidden bedrooms, sunken tubs, fruit orchards, and private lakes. . .that is, if it hasn't been sold again.

Take a break for cocktails and lunch at Bonnie Springs Ranch, next stop on Highway 159. The wood-clapped structure was built in 1843 for travelers crossing the Mohave Desert on their way to California. That was all Las Vegas was meant to be in the first place — just a short-cut to L.A. and back. A young Mexican scout discovered the area in 1829, and the Paiute Indians — who had lived here since 1500 — said, ''Well, there goes the neighborhood.''

Wild burros amble across the road, stopping motorists with pleading eyes. More wildlife abounds at the Bonnie Springs Petting Zoo, including baby lambs and buffalo. Across a rickety bridge is the town of Old Nevada, a faithful re-creation of a frontier town from the late 1800s. There are mock gunfights in the streets, silent movies at the Bijou, and plenty of shops. Outside, a miniature train snakes around the village, and for just a moment the 20th century seems a long way off.

Fifty-five miles northeast of Las Vegas is Valley Of Fire, Nevada's oldest state park (Interstate 15 and watch for turnoff). The 26,000-acre park got its name because of the effects of sunlight on the reddish rock formations, many of which are named for the things they resemble: Beehive Rock, Elephant Rock, and Poodle Rock among others. The most legendary area is Mouse's Tank, a hidden can-yon a quarter of a mile through soft yielding sand. Mouse was a renegade Indian, and his tank was a small pothole of water. When miners came to drink, Mouse would bush-whack them. Eventually he was apprehended, but his story lives on. Prehistoric Indians first inhabited the region 25,000 years ago, and left their history in the form of petroglyphs — pictures etched in sandstone. Primitive graffiti it may be, but it is still a bit more exotic than: "Kilroy was here."

South of Valley of Fire is the Lost City Museum in Overton. Over a half century ago, ancient Indian villages of the Anasazi were unearthed along the Muddy River, hence the name "Lost City." The tribe emerged before Christ, at a time when Rome dominated northern Europe. Later descendants, primarily Pueblo Indians, introduced agriculture to the area in 1000 A.D.

Lake Mead & Hoover Dam

From Overton, the road south follows the blue-scrubbed surface of Lake Mead, largest man-made body of water in the United States. The Lake Mead Recreation Area encompasses 1.4 million acres of scenery, wildlife, and history. Created by Hoover Dam, the lake is an outside funhouse for swimmers, boaters, skiiers, and fishermen. There are six major marinas and three resorts on the water's edge, including the Echo Bay Resort just outside Overton.

Since fishing is allowed year-round, Lake Mead is one of the few places in the country where anglers can cast their bait to the wind for: bass, trout, crappie, bluegill, catfish and even silver salmon. There are also plenty of carp in the water, who will thrash themselves into a frenzy for a handful of popcorn.

Before Hoover Dam was built (1931-1935), the 1,400-mile long Colorado River was a raging torrent that wiped out everything in its path. At other times, it would shrivel to a trickle under the harsh desert sun. Then came the dam, the mighty steel-lined 70-stories-high concrete dam. It backed up the Colorado, which had cut through the Grand Canyon like a hot knife, and Lake Mead came to be. Electricity was generated, enough to juice up Arizona, California, and Nevada. Arched over a narrow pass in Black Canyon, Hoover Dam is a wondrous example of man's triumph over nature.

Seven miles away is Boulder City. Originally a government camp for construction crews that built Hoover Dam, the town hugs the Lake Mead shoreline like an old blanket. The city was designed, laid out, developed and administered by the Bureau of Reclamation, and consequently is considered America's first planned community. The only thing that was not planned was the name of the dam. First it was called Boulder Dam, so it was only natural to name the town Boulder City. Then in 1947, Congress decided to honor Herbert Hoover so Boulder Dam became Hoover Dam. Apparently, the vacuum cleaner wasn't enough.

Although Boulder City is only a holler away from Las Vegas, the cities are complete opposites. Boulder City prides itself on its "clean, green" image, and is the only city in Nevada where gambling is illegal. One of the finest hotels in the West is located there — the stately Boulder Dam Hotel. It was built in 1933 to play host to visiting dignitaries who toured the dam, including Franklin Roosevelt. So what is the hotel best remembered for? Why, it's where Clark Gable and Carole Lombard spent their honeymoon!

A Day Away

North of Las Vegas about 120 miles (on U.S. Highway 95) is the old mining camp of Rhyolite. At the turn of the century, there were 8,000 people panning for gold in this windswept place. Scanty veins of the precious ore played out, and the miners moved on. Still, there is something about a ghost town that quickens the heartbeat and stirs the soul.

Just up the dusty highway is the turnoff to Death Valley, a national monument claimed by both Nevada and California. (Nevada claims it's in California; California claims it's in Nevada.) To a viewer's eye, it would seem as though God blinked for a moment when He was creating the universe, though actually Death Valley was the result of constant erosion and faulting.

Further into Death Valley, the road dips low on the desert floor. Hot, dry salt flats are punctuated by grotesque shapes wavering in the heat: Hell's Gate, Dante's View, the Devil's Golf Course, Bad Water. The latter is the lowest point in the country, 282 feet below sea level. Then there is Manly's Beacon, Golden Canyon, Red Cathedral, Telescope Peak, and Zabriskie Point. A short distance from Zabriskie Point is Furnace Creek Ranch, with actual grass growing out of the ground. At the ranch, shadowed by a grove of date palms, is the Borax Museum and all that is left of the 20 Mule Team Borax mineral works.

RV owners come by the thousands every November for "Death Valley Days," a celebration to boggle the mind with fiddling contests, square dancing, and just plain old goofing off. For *non*-RV owners, it is a good time to go to the Grand Canyon instead.

The Grand Canyon is less than a day's drive from Las Vegas. One of the seven natural wonders of the world, this scenic masterpiece can also be reached from Vegas by chartered bus ($88), airplane ($125), and helicopter ($200). Once there, other modes of transportation are procurable. You can ride a mule to the bottom of the mile-deep canyon; you can bob in a raft down the Colorado River; you can use your feet to walk, hike, climb, jog, saunter, stroll and run; and you can use your fingers to phone for an ambulance after slipping, sliding, stumbling and tumbling.

Accommodations and camping are available on both the north rim and the more accessible south rim of the Grand Canyon. The views are like living postcards, although it is difficult to comprehend the utter vastness of this place half as old as the earth itself.

The best times for viewing the canyon's gorges and mesas are early morning and late afternoon. Wildlife buffs will find plenty of chipmunks, squirrels and mule deer. And yes, kids, there's a MacDonald's in Grand Canyon Village.

Closer to Las Vegas is Cedar Breaks, about four hours northeast on Interstate 15 (exit at Cedar City, Utah). This natural amphitheater was carved out of sandstone by frost and trickling water, and the result is a view that makes time stand still. All that is missing are the cedar trees for which this national monument was named. Mormon pioneers thought the scaly-needled trees around these parts were cedars, but they turned out to be junipers. Oh well, we all make mistakes.

From Cedar Breaks, State Highway 14 heads southeast through the Dixie National Forest to Long Valley Junction.

Before reaching the junction, however, there are dozens of delightful detours. Route 143 takes you past Panguitch Lake and the mountain community of Brian Head to Parowan, and the main road back to Vegas. Or stay on 14 and climb to an altitude of 10,000 feet near majestic Navajo Lake. Look for the turnoff, which also leads to Cascade Falls. There a moderate hike finds you standing on a wooden bridge within spray's touch of a roaring waterfall.

From Long Valley Junction the road goes north to Bryce Canyon National Park via Red Canyon, or south to Mt. Carmel and Zion National Park. Bryce Canyon, with 60 miles of hiking trails branching off a 20-mile main road, is full of what locals call "hoodoos" — spires and arches that in the moonlight resemble ghostly hooded figures. Sky-high sandstone steeples are the soup du jour at Zion, which is reached by going through a scary mile-long tunnel at the face of Pine Creek Canyon. The scenery at Zion almost inspires religious reverence. Jagged pinnacles bear names like Great Arch of Zion, East Temple, Great White Throne, Three Patriarchs, and Angels Landing...so called because early explorers predicted only winged angels could ever set foot on top.

Brothels

Now that we finally have your attention, did you know that Nevada is the only state with legalized brothels? Of course, there are a few restrictions. It is at county option, and in rural areas...which lets out Clark and Washoe counties. There are 37 houses of ill repute in the state, with such ethereal names as My Place, Lucky Strike, Cotton Tail Ranch, Pussycat, and Penny's Cozy Corner. And:

Doll House, Club Mona Lisa, Mona's 2, Kit Kat Ranch, Villa Joy, Simone de Paris, Calico Club, and the Mustang Ranch.

Closer to Las Vegas are the Chicken Ranch and Sheri's Patch, both in Pahrump; Bobby's Buckeye Bar in Tonopah; the Cherry Patch in Crystal Springs; the Valley of Dolls in Lathrop Wells; and Fran's Star Ranch in Beatty. Ladies of the night who are employed in such establishments are referred to as "prostitutes." (PROS-tuh-toots)

In the town of Wells, prostitutes can only do their shopping between 8 a.m. and 5 p.m. They are not allowed to dine in public restaurants unless they are accompanied by a brothel manager, and they cannot bathe while "seminude." They are not allowed to dress in an alluring manner, and if going on vacation they "must use the most expeditious transport out of Wells." Who knows? Maybe that is how the human cannonball got started.

Brothels in Nevada range from small operations with two or three girls to the notorious Mustang Ranch complex near Reno, where 100 women and eight bartenders are employed. With the recent AIDS scare, brothels would seem to be a thing of the past, but not so. To date, not a single case of the dreaded disease has been traced to a Nevada bordello. That is one reason why the state's 400 prostitutes undergo weekly testing. . .to take the worry out of being close.

CHAPTER 12

Thanks For The Memories

You can imagine how I felt when I saw the envelope in my mailbox. "Sands Las Vegas" was written in fancy script up in the left hand corner, and under that it said "35 Years of Tradition."

"Dear Friend," the letter read, "the Sands Resort and Casino is pleased to have you be a part of our 35th Anniversary Celebration!" I could not believe my good fortune. Me, a guy who worked in a Texas cotton gin when the Sands opened in 1952, being invited to hobnob with a bunch of movie stars and dignitaries. I mean, the cream of society was going to be there, and I could not even find the pants to my dark blue suit.

This was special. Who among us does not remember the celebrated Copa Room, where the impromptu "Rat Pack" was formed. The names roll off the tongue without even a nudge from the brain: Sinatra, Joey Bishop, Sammy Davis Jr., Peter Lawford, Dean Martin. It was true, the Sands Hotel was the original Tiffany of the Strip, and I was going to help sing "happy birthday."

I read the letter again. "On Saturday, November 14, show business legend Bob Hope will be entertaining for a private party in the famed Grand Ballroom. This special party will be a very sentimental occasion attended by celebrities who have performed on the Sands Copa Room stage throughout the years.''

I did not know it at the time, but 35 years ago in Las Vegas two casinos opened that changed the whole complexion of the Strip. The Club Bingo (later to be called the Sahara) was one, and the other was the Sands. In those days, a fledgling resort was nothing more than a motel, spread out on barren sand that stretched as far as the eye could see. Oldtimers will even tell you what was there before the Sands — it was LaRue's Restaurant (Coffee 5 cents, Refills Free), and The Kit Carson Motel stood where the Sands parking lot is now.

Don't get me wrong. I don't want to take anything away from the Flamingo's claim as the first big resort on the Strip. Bugsy Siegel spent almost all the mob's money in 1946 to build what was then the classiest casino in town, but people were more interested in seeing him than his hotel. It was even rumored that Bugsy fertilized his Flamingo rose garden with members of rival gangs, which were always a ''thorn'' in his side. Wilbur Clark then built the Desert Inn in 1950, and that started all the hoopla about Las Vegas being the entertainment capital of the world.

It was the Sands, though, that had always offered the ultimate in show biz, beginning with Danny Thomas who opened the Copa Room on December 15, 1952, with ''Danny Boy.'' So when I came to Las Vegas in 1967 this was my first stop. By then the Sands had that wonderful little 17-story tower that looked like it was made out of gingerbread, and the surprisingly small neon sign out front. THE SANDS logo was written in longhand across it, with the ''S'' done in a huge flair, and under that: ''A Place In The Sun.''

It really was. The inside of the casino was almost hushed, the softly subdued lighting echoing off real wood paneling, nothing at all like that stuff they sell at K Mart. Along the walls were hung the portraits of all the superstars who graced the stage of the Copa Room: Nat King Cole, George Burns, Jerry Lewis, Red Skelton, Milton Berle, and on and on. Jack Entratter was in charge of entertainment, and his name was always on the marquee.

Jack Entratter Presents
DEAN MARTIN
MAYBE FRANK   MAYBE SAMMY

"The stars not only appeared at the Sands," said hotel president Patrick Cruzen, "but many were married here, vacationed here, or just dropped in to relax and enjoy the atmosphere." Old black and white photos tell the story: Jimmy Durante ringside with Maurice Chevalier and Danny Kaye, all gone now; Humphrey Bogart standing over wife Lauren with Judy Garland sitting next to her; Jerry Lewis standing over a low-cut Jayne Mansfield and trying to look at something besides Jayne Mansfield; a young, snappy John Kennedy impatiently waiting for the camera's click; Marilyn Monroe seated all alone and looking like a crisp platinum flower; Dick Haymes marrying Rita Hayworth; Henry Fonda and Kirk Douglas swapping grins; Harry Truman playing the piano; and Tony Curtis with dark hair, all mementos of a time gone by.

In fact, I saw my very first celebrity at the Sands. It was in the Regency Room, the chic cafe and watering hole just off the main casino. I went in the bar for a nightcap, and there, less than fifteen feet away, holding court like King

Arthur (and indeed he nearly was) sat the idol of my youth. It was Frank Sinatra, at the head of a long table crowded with others of lesser stature. I am almost embarrassed to admit this, but I stared at Sinatra so long that he finally began staring back at *me*, and I have never really forgiven him for that.

You have to remember that in the '60s Frank Sinatra was to Las Vegas what orange juice is to Florida. He not only performed at the Sands, but he also had some ownership points in the place. This gave him the right to many privileges, which included taking markers at the gaming tables. When Howard Hughes bought the Sands in 1967, those liberties were stopped and that's when Frank Sinatra stopped belting songs and tried belting a pit boss.

As the story goes, he was piling up his usual maze of markers and stuffing the chips in his pockets when one of the casino bosses cut off his credit. To Sinatra, Vegas was no longer "My Kind Of Town," and that is when he did "Something Stupid." He hopped on a bellman's golf cart, crashing right through a plate-glass window. He tore up his room, tore out telephone lines, and tore verbally into every casino big shot in sight. Then he left the hotel.

Two days later he returned, going woodenly from boss to boss and reciting as though by memory a brief apology to all concerned. An eyewitness said that Sinatra then went to the lounge, where he stewed and got stewed until early the next morning. Word reached casino boss Carl Cohen that Sinatra was at the bar. So Cohen, who had been out of town during the skirmish two days before, went to see the singer in an effort to smooth things over.

During the conversation, Sinatra became more belligerent and finally threw a punch at Cohen. Apparently no one had told Frank that Carl Cohen once drove a beer truck in Cleveland and could toss a crate of Budweiser right up there with the best of them. It was one of those instances of "Fly Me To The Moon." Sinatra never finished his punch. He wound up limping out of the lounge minus the caps on his two front teeth, never again to perform at the Sands. From there he went to Caesars Palace for a long stay, later to the Golden Nugget, and currently he performs at Bally's.

A retired Sands pit boss remembers when Sinatra ordered all the lemon meringue pies in the coffee shop sent to the health club, where he was getting a back massage. "Everybody that walked into the health spa got a pie in the face. Well, it was funny except that it almost ended Frank's career. Jack Entratter walked in. Jack was a big man, six four in his bare feet, and he had spent his youth as a bouncer at the Copacabana. He saw the pie coming and he turned his head, getting it right in the ear. He walked around all day saying 'huh?' until a doctor finally got all the meringue out of his ear. Then he went up to Frank and said, 'If you ever do that again, I will kill you. I will beat you to death.' It was one of the few times in his life that Sinatra said 'Yes sir.' "

Red Skelton was a "slot machine freak," according to Sands assistant maitre d' Neil Ohriner. In fact, one of the conditions in Red's contract with Jack Entratter was that a slot machine be placed in his dressing room and another in his suite. One afternoon he was playing a quarter slot machine at the hotel, surrounded by fans who were amazed at his run of good luck. Every time Red pulled the handle he hit a jackpot, no matter what came up on the reels. Two lemons and a plum, jackpot. A watermelon and two bars, jackpot. Orange, plum, 7, jackpot. What the fans did not know was that Skelton, always the practical joker, had a pocket bulging with quarters. As soon as he spun the reels he would toss a handful of coins into the metal tray. When Skelton finally walked away there was a mad dash by onlookers to play the same slot machine, while Red laughed all the way to his room.

"Find a penny, pick it up. All day long you'll have good luck." We've all heard that old chestnut, but to Red Skelton this was Commandment Number Eleven. Neil Ohriner tells the story:

"Red is very superstitious, one of those eccentric millionaires who walks around with his head down, always looking to find a penny. Probably two or three times a week we would 'seed' the Copa Room with pennies. After the first show Red always walked out through the showroom, and we knew which aisle he was going to use. Well, when he found one he was like a three-year-old boy with a 20-pound bag of lollipops. He would giggle and laugh and show us this penny he'd found. And we would always say, 'Gee, Red, are you lucky!'

"He always wanted a standing ovation after his show. When he took his final bow his hands would appear to come up involuntarily from his sides, and 90 percent of the time it was enough to bring the crowd to its feet. Red would come off the stage and say to me, 'Look at all those dodos standing up.' If the crowd did not give him a standing ovation he would say to me, 'Look at all those dodos sitting down.' "

Ohriner said one of the funniest moments he remembers was the time Sonny King accidentally banged his microphone against the ceiling while performing in the lounge. "The microphone hit one of the sprinklers and set off all the fire alarms in the casino. The sprinklers in the lounge came on, and all the people were sitting there getting wet and probably thinking it was all part of the act. Then I heard Sonny croon, 'I'm singing in the rain, just singing in the rain...' "

One of the biggest fans of the grand old Sands is U.S. Senator Chic Hecht of Nevada. "It was the hotel that started Las Vegas on the big time," he says. "It was the first hotel that brought big entertainers and it's the hotel that really skyrocketed this town. It was swanky. It had the best food in town. All the best high rollers came here. I remember walking through the casino and seeing nothing but black $100 chips on the tables. All the casino bosses knew all the customers. It was a very, very personal place."

I learned through the grapevine that Senator Hecht was going to be at the Sands birthday party, along with Bob Hope and all the others. My only concern was how I should pose for the photographers. Should I be smiling with Bob Hope talking, or should I be talking with Bob Hope smiling, or should we both be smiling, or what? Well, I would work that out later.

Darkness fell, and with one last glimpse in the mirror I headed for the Sands Hotel. I didn't bother with valet parking, opting instead for Denny's next door. It was not the 25 cents for the parking attendant that discouraged me, but the fact that with all those movie stars going through the front entrance I might never get my car back, and my VW bus was almost a collector's item.

For one thing, I was not big on fighting crowds. Working in a casino for twenty years had cured me of standing in line anywhere. And for some reason, every time I saw a celebrity I came away a little disappointed. They were either too tall or too short, too young or too old.

Now here I was, getting ready to meet a whole platoon of these people. It made me wonder, with some alarm, if

Frank Sinatra was going to be there. If so, would he remember that I was the one who stared at him in the Regency Room? That made me start hoping that dessert tonight was not going to be lemon meringue pie.

Regardless of all the jokes, though, Sinatra was the one who put the Sands on the map. It was like a fellow entertainer described him to me, "Frank is an old man. He's not good looking, he certainly can't sing. But when he gets up on that stage and points his finger at the audience, everybody is plugged into 220. He has that certain charisma that very few people have."

I went through the door of the Sands and caught the blast of a thousand slot machines having dinner. Straight ahead was the Copa Room, remodeled now, and not the same. Performing in there tonight was somebody called "The Checkmates," whose only claim to fame was that they sounded like "Stark Naked and the Car Thieves."

It was certainly a far cry from the summits of Sinatra, when the show was always good and exactly one hour and twenty minutes long. "In those days, that's the way it was," Neil Ohriner told me. "Those were the rules. Get the people in, give them an hour and twenty, and get them back in the casino. Well, Frank had an interest in the hotel. The longer he kept them in, the less money he was going to make in the casino."

Quality, not quantity, was what made it better back then when you could sit there in the audience and smoke a cigarette without offending someone, and watch a living American legend like Jimmy Durante, so close you could almost reach out and touch him. "He was like an old car," Ohriner laughed. "He had a valet who used to give him a body rub to get him going before his show. Once he got all that blood moving, he would go out on that stage and do his thing. People couldn't believe how this wonderful old guy could move around, but he had to get his motor started for every show.''

A former showroom captain at the Sands recalled Joe E. Lewis with fondness, describing the legendary comic as "such a gentle man, who never hurt a person in his life." Lewis had two great loves during his lifetime: his audience, and Ambassador 12 Scotch. "He would sit down ringside, when he came to see another performer, and order a quart of Ambassador 12. He didn't like fifths, he felt he was being cheated with fifths. And however long the show lasted, that's how long the quart lasted.''

I was wondering if maybe Joey Bishop was going to be there tonight. He was big in the '60s, starting to fade in the '70s, and his career by the '80s had gone to Hades. An ex-boss of the Sands tells the story: "Joey Bishop had a TV show up against Johnny Carson, and it bombed. Finally the network dropped him, paying off his contract which was up in the millions.

"So the week the news hit the papers Joey came to the Sands to spend a few days. He's sitting in the showroom talking to Jack Entratter and Danny Thomas, and Jack asks him what he's going to do. 'Well Jack, I'm buying myself a big boat, and I'm just going to relax and enjoy life.' Danny Thomas lit into Joey like a father lecturing his son. 'Joey, you have to work. You've got to show the world you're just as funny as ever, because if you don't stay up there the public is going to forget you.' Bishop shook his head no. 'When I decide to come back,' he said, 'I'll come back.' He never did. He tried twice, but he never did.''

By now I was walking past the Regency Room, which once upon a time was called The Garden Room. Before the tower was built, it was the only restaurant in the whole hotel, with a snack bar stuck on the outside that serviced the pool area. When "Oceans 11" was being filmed in Las Vegas, Sinatra and clan would eat there between scenes.

"Frank was a simple eater," Ohriner had told me. "No sauces, no gravies, and he didn't like anyone upsetting his dinner." Peter Lawford was giving everybody a hard time one night, repeatedly asking for more water and then calling the captain over to complain about his steak. "I wanted it medium-rare, but this is more on the medium side than the rare side." Sinatra overheard him and put down his silverware. "What did you say?" he roared. "Eat that steak before I personally shove it down your throat." There was silence for a moment, then Lawford began eating and the others followed suit.

Up ahead loomed the Grand Ballroom of the Sands. So far I had not seen one single celebrity, but the foyer in front of me was bathed in harsh light and I could see television cameras grinding away as each guest entered. I adjusted my tie and made my way inside. The lights suddenly went off as I came through the door, as though the cameramen realized that "Hey, this guy is a dodo."

People were milling around with drinks in their hands, and they were all strangers to me. There were two bars set up on either side of the room, and through another open doorway I could see the cavernous Grand Ballroom. An orchestra was tuning up and there was a huge caricature of "old ski nose" draped behind the bandstand. I headed glumly for the nearest bartender and got myself a drink, then whiled away a few minutes looking at "8x10" glossies thumbtacked to particle board like old animal skins.

The Sands had really changed since the last time I had been there. A person almost needed a road map to find his way around, and it struck me as rather sad. The only thing I knew for sure was that tonight's celebration was a swan song of sorts for the Summa Corporation, which had already agreed to sell the Sands and all their other hotels to somebody else. That, and where the hell *was* everybody?

"Hey, Barney!" I heard my name being called and turned with a start. Someone who looked distantly familiar was headed toward me, a drink in his hand. He had a moustache, so it was not Dean Martin. It was my friend Sergio Lalli with the local newspaper.

He was in the company of a couple of attractive older ladies who turned out to be about my age. Once introductions were exchanged, I learned they were original Copa Girls, part of a fabulous chorus line sharing the stage with Sands headliners throughout the years. One of the ladies said she did not even know how to dance when she was hired. "Jack Entratter told us that all we needed was to be beautiful, and that he would teach us how to dance." The other lady added that the chorus line never went topless. "Jack wanted us to be sexy but ladylike. We mainly showed lots of legs."

I learned later that bare-chested showgirls did not become a Las Vegas tradition until 1957, when Major Riddle brought the first French-style revue to the Dunes. (It is hard to keep abreast of everything that goes on in this crazy town.)

Sergio and I made our way into the ballroom, where we located our table wedged up against the service door. A crowd of approximately 500 people was already seated, knives and forks rattling as dinner was served.

"Did you see anybody?" I asked Sergio.

"They're all over the place," he replied, checking his salad for insects.

"Like — who?"

"Bernie Allen, Edd Byrnes, Foster Brooks, Oran Gragson, you name it."

"I was thinking more along the lines of Frank Sinatra, Lucille Ball, Red Skelton, Danny Thomas, you name it."

"I talked to somebody about getting an interview with Bob Hope," Sergio said, "but he's getting here late."

"How about after the show?"

"He's leaving early."

"Oh."

"Yeah."

"The invitation said all the stars who played at the Sands were going to be here. Maybe they're in a private section, or something."

"A lot of them couldn't make it," Sergio answered. "The maitre d' told me Patti Page was here."

"Where?"

"Front table. On the left."

I grabbed my notebook and started shouldering my way to the front of the ballroom. I had always admired Patti Page, ever since she did "Wheel Of Fortune." Or was that Kay Starr? But there were other songs: "Cross Over The Bridge," "Tennessee Waltz." I even remembered her nickname: The Singing Rage, Miss Patti Page.

She was sitting there, gazing pensively at the stage, and I introduced myself. What can I tell you, she was just as beautiful as ever, almost serene in the knowledge that she was the grand priestess of the Top 20, back before there was such a thing as rock and roll. Maybe she was not in the same class as Sinatra and Martin, but at least she was here.

"Just a couple of questions," I pleaded.

"All right."

"What is your fondest memory of the Sands?"

"I played here three times a year during the 1960s. I had two small children, a daughter and a son. Jack Entratter put me in a private suite with its own little swimming pool. He even furnished me with a rocking chair, so I could rock my babies to sleep at night." A pause, and then, "I wonder if they still have that rocking chair in some old storage room somewhere."

I was scribbling as fast as I could, cursing myself for never learning shorthand. "Uhh, what are you doing now that you have retired?"

She recoiled, and for an instant I was afraid I had accidentally poked her with my ballpoint. "I *haven't* retired," she said stiffly.

Suddenly the lights dimmed, and — saying my goodbyes — I headed back to my table just in time to see my meal disappear in the hands of a six-foot waitress. I asked Sergio what we had for dinner. "Steak and lobster," he said. "It was pretty good."

"Oh."

"Yeah."

All at once the orchestra broke into that famous theme song "Thanks For The Memories." A sprightly man walked briskly onstage while an announcer said, "Ladies and gentlemen, Mister Bob Hope!" As the crowd rose, little sketches of Bob Hope whirled through my head... listening to Bob Hope on the car radio while my dad drove the old Hudson, seeing "The Lemon Drop Kid" with Bob Hope in San Antonio while my dad ate all my popcorn. How I wished he was with me now, but some things were never meant to be.

My melancholy mood was swept away as Hope went into his routine: "I love the Sands. It's a family hotel. I know, because every guy in the lobby is with his niece." (Laughter) "They put me up in a super suite. It even had a mirror over the bed." (Laughter) "Of course, I didn't know what it was for." (Laughter and applause) "But it was nice, lying there and watching myself shave." (Laughter) "I had to fly in from Hollywood." (Giggles) "I called the airlines and asked, 'Can you guarantee I'll be in Las Vegas by eight o'clock?' And they said, 'Only if you're calling from there.' " (Laughter) "But I want you to know that I've got a new makeup crew." (Applause) "The guys that restored the Statue of Liberty." (Applause and laughter) "And I have to work." (Catcalls) "No, seriously." (Laughter, whistles) "I lost a bundle on Joan Crawford Day Care Centers." (Laughter, applause, chair scraping, foot stomping)

The rest of it was a blur, and now the orchestra was playing "Buttons And Bows" and — just like that — Bob Hope was gone. Then the band broke into "Happy Birthday" and out was wheeled a cake the size of Rhode Island. If I were Bob Hope I would have said, "This cake is so big that the candles on top are in a different time zone." (Boos, hisses, Bronx cheers, tomato throwing.)

The crowd was on its feet again, and I was one of them this time. I am not ashamed to tell you I had tears in my eyes as I stood on legs that wobbled like old fence posts. I was so — hungry. But there was more to it than that. I felt almost as though I had drifted back through time, and that Nat King Cole was still playing the piano somewhere. If only they had kept the magic, this town could have really been something. Oh well, that's progress for you.

Thanks, Sands. Thanks for the memories. Now can I have my steak and lobster back?

CHAPTER 13

International Gaming

Gambling is nothing new. Spain has been having a national lottery for 225 years, and it is the richest game of its kind in the world. Over $750 million was given away during the recent "El Gordo" (Fatso) Sweepstakes, and cash winners included such diversified interests as a banana vendor, a bishop, and the City Hall in Soria. The annual event comes during the Christmas holidays, which explains why Yuletide goodies are stuffed inside pinatas instead of stockings. Since everyone spends their money on lottery tickets, all their socks have holes in them.

Spain is just one of 70 nations around the world where gambling is legal. As one gaming consultant said, however, "Europe may be saturated. The Middle East may be frightening, Africa may seem unfriendly, and South America may be unstable." That leaves the Unites States — and Australia.

Thanks to Australian gaming writer John Beagle, we are able to give you a thumbnail sketch of gambling "down under." Of course, Beagle may be prejudiced. His definition of Australia: "Beautiful one day, perfect the next."

Australia's island state of Tasmania was the site of the country's first legal casino, when the West Point Federal

Hotel opened in 1973. Since that time, casinos — limited by law to one in each locality — have sprung up in Alice Springs, Darwin, Adelaide, Perth, Townsville and just outside Brisbane on Queensland's Gold Coast.

According to Beagle, "The major difference between Australian casinos and those in the United States is that Australian casinos exist for the city and its population, rather than the city existing for the casinos and the visitors they attract."

In Australia, people have been gambling since the nation was founded in 1788. In fact, Australia is the only country in the world to celebrate a national holiday based on a horse race, the million-dollar purse Melbourne Cup. Casino games are the same as their American counterparts, except for the Australian national "favourite" of Two-Up Ring.

From the Burswood Casino Gaming Guide:

"The person who is chosen to spin (the "Spinner") by the croupier ringkeeper shall spin for "Heads" only (both coins showing heads). The "Spinner" then chooses two coins and places them on the kip, "Tails" side up and then when called by the ringkeeper, spins the coins at least one metre above his head. Both coins must spin or else this is known as a "floater" and the spin becomes invalid. To win, the "Spinner" must spin heads three times before spinning Tails or 5 consecutive "Odds" (1 Head and 1 Tail). If the "Spinner" spins heads 3 times, he will be paid at odds of 7 and a half to 1. If not, he retires from the ring."

And he wonders why this game hasn't caught on in Las Vegas!

Australia allows anyone over the age of 18 to gamble, and more than two-thirds of the patrons are local residents.

The economy gets a nice jolt, because major casinos pay as much as 20 percent in state gaming taxes, along with normal federal taxes. There is no credit gambling in Australian casinos, and winnings are *non-taxable*. As far as working conditions are concerned, tips are not allowed, but there are other fringe benefits to keep employees happy.

Salaries for dealers are higher than they are in this country, around $23,000 per year. Any dealer with over ten years experience gets three months of vacation. Dealers who work after 7 p.m. or on Sundays and holidays are paid "penalty" rates ranging from extra pay to double pay. Employees also enjoy pensions and paid sick leave, something that Las Vegas dealers can only dream about.

Since the American dollar is worth more in Australia, many gamblers from the U.S. are being attracted to this bold country of 16 million. The Diamond Beach Casino in Darwin will pay full expenses for a high-rolling gambler from anywhere in the world, provided he spends four nights at the tables. Darwin presently charters regular flights from Singapore with graded complimentaries for all ranges of players. The program is so successful that there are constant waiting lists for such flights.

The biggest threat to Nevada gaming is not Australia, however, but the Caribbean. Gaming expert Mike Sloan of Circus Circus says, "If the U.S. becomes the only country in the world that makes gaming winnings taxable, offshore casinos will boom." (Legislation taxing foreign gamblers on their winnings has been pending in the United States for several years.)

Resorts International, with its Paradise Island Casino in the Bahamas, is already bringing high rollers in by the planeloads. Add Miami cruise ships to that, and it is easy to visualize this bustling new network of 55 casinos in 32 localities. Profits are sluggish — about $300 million annually — yet the outlook is as bright as the Caribbean sun.

"I don't think a lot of the casino operators there had the credibility in the beginning that they have now," said World Gaming Technology vice-president Barry Quick. "But major corporations now operating in the Bahamas are comparable to anything you will find in the states. The Caribbean is not a gambling destination like Las Vegas. It's an aditional form of entertainment.

"Most of the operations don't open until four o'clock in the afternoon, and in reality most of the income is made from 8 p.m. until 1 a.m." The only problem with the Caribbean, according to Quick, is that there may be too much too soon. "I have to believe there has been too much casino expansion in some areas of the Caribbean," Quick said, "fueled understandably by local governments trying to stimulate additional investments and employment for the locals."

The Ramada Corporation does not agree. It cites record tourist arrivals, especially in Puerto Rico and Grand Bahama. "We're expanding as fast as we can," said Nikolas Eastwick-Field, vice-president of Ramada's Latin America and Caribbean division. "Latin America and the Caribbean ended up being the last part of the world where Ramada had no representation. It was an obvious place where we had to go."

Ramada is presently pursuing projects in Antigua, the Bahamas, St. Croix, the Cayman Islands, and Curacao. Although the region has a reputation for instability, Eastwick-Field said, "I think there is much more understanding of the importance of tourism in this area." Accordingly, Ramada expects to have 20 hotels and 5,000 rooms open in Latin America and the Caribbean within the next few years. Ten of those will be off the coast of Florida.

After all, international gaming is big business. International Game Technology in Reno, which claims to be the largest producer of slot machines in the world, is already exporting one-fourth of its new machines every year to such markets as Turkey, France and Australia. The forecast is for this figure to skyrocket as slot machines become more and more popular overseas.

IGT even has slot machines on cruise ships, including 76 machines on the world's largest luxury liner "Sovereign of the Seas." Atlantic Maritime Services has the gambling concession for Royal Cruise Lines, Holland American, Sitmar, Regency Cruises, and Sea Escape. Casinos on board these ships offer standard table games such as blackjack, craps, and roulette, as well as slot machines "by the hundreds," according to vice-president Earl Ziplow. One would think that since a cruise ship has a captive audience, the machines would not be as loose as those in U.S. casinos. Not so. Said Ziplow, "Our hold is set at the factory by Bally, and we use the same casino models as Las Vegas and Atlantic City."

That can be misleading, however, since statutes differ in U.S. markets. "There's a flat law in Atlantic City," said a slot manufacturer, "that each machine must give a minimum per-customer payback of 83 percent. There is no such law in Las Vegas, but if a machine is too tight the control board might kick it back to the manufacturer. I would say, though, that they're more or less set up along the same lines as the Caribbean and Atlantic City." If such is the case, then dollar slot machines on cruise ships pay back between 87 and 93 percent, while quarter machines pay back around 85 percent. In other words, it is all right to gamble on cruise ships, but don't go overboard.

A recent survey showed that there are nine cruise ship lines with some type of legalized gambling. There are over 500 casinos scattered around the world, from Argentina to Zimbabwe and most points in between. Twenty-six states in the U.S. have lotteries, as well as 85 different countries including Czechoslovakia, Sri Lanka, and the Soviet Union. Put in this perspective, Las Vegas seems to lose a little of its luster. Gaming consultant Nigel Kent-Lemon phrased it in a few choice words when he said, "Las Vegas is unique as a destination resort, and always will be. But now gambling centers such as Las Vegas are being set up all over the world."

England boasted gaming houses as far back as the 18th and early 19th centuries. When Queen Victoria came to rule, however, she did something that few monarchs had done before her. She enforced the laws. Suddenly gaming houses turned into private clubs, and no one could gain entry without a membership. And how did a person become a member? He opened the door and walked inside, preferably with English currency scotch-taped to his forehead. By 1968, there were over 1,200 private clubs in Great Britain. The clubs advertised, brought in their own junkets, and did other things that would eventually incur the wrath of parliament.

"Meyer Lansky shifted his attentions to London after Fidel Castro closed his Havana casinos," wrote gaming expert William Thompson. "But parliament knew that they had a problem greater than just a few foreign characters. Corruption was rampant. A crackdown was demanded."

As a result, England's Gaming Control Board was set

up in 1968 with the responsibility of licensing "owners of good character, free of organized crime connections, adequately financed and sufficiently familiar with gambling to be successful." By 1987 there were 120 casinos left in England, 20 of those in London, and a few other changes as well.

Advertising has been prohibited, new club members must wait 48 hours before gambling for the first time, no drinking is allowed, and each casino — confined to cities with over 150,000 population — is allowed only two slot machines. Then again, for every law there seems to be a loophole.

"Every pub has a form of slot machine," Barry Quick explained. "It is called an AWP, or 'amusement with prize.' The maximum payout is a pound and a half (about $1.60), but it has spinning reels and is essentially a slot machine. There are probably 400,000 of those machines in the U.K."

Somewhere else where slot machines proliferate are at U.S. servicemen's clubs, but only in countries where gambling is legal. According to a gaming consultant (who must remain anonymous because of his dealings with regulatory agencies), the slot machines were originally installed in army clubs during the Korean war. Everyone got rich off the venture, except the servicemen — and the army. The machines wound up being dumped in the ocean, and the whole thing was forgotten. Then an army officer approached the Secretary of Defense about reinstituting slot machine gaming, and a field test was made in Germany.

Now there are over 5,000 slot machines at officer's and enlisted men's clubs from Germany to Italy to Panama to

Korea to Japan. "Profits last year were in excess of $14 million," the consultant said. "These are non-appropriated funds, not one dime from the taxpayers. And the only one who doesn't know about it is Congress."

Germany was the perfect spot to do a field test on slot machines. After all, gambling had flourished there as early as 1720. It was legalized in Bad Kissingen in 1756, in Baden Baden in 1748, and in Wiesbaden in 1771. By 1800, there were 24 casinos in Germany, but when the southwestern region of Germany was unified with Prussia in 1872, gambling was finally outlawed.

After World War II the casinos finally reopened, thanks to the leniency of occupying armies. Then came a land-mark decision by Chancellor Konrad Adenauer. Gambling came under the jurisdiction of individual states. William Thompson wrote:

"Americans must have been relieved by the opinion. Our Marshall Plan had financed the opening of the casino at Travemunde, the only casino on the Baltic today. Ironically, we provided that funding at the same time voices were being heard in Washington calling for the end of gaming in Nevada."

French roulette is the dominant game in German casinos, as it is elsewhere in Europe. The reason is cultural. It was the first game that was available, so it has always been popular. Less fashionable, but more profitable for the casino, is *American* roulette... sporting not only a single zero, but a *double* zero as well! Good ol' American greed. Since patrons expect silence inside their casinos, slot machines are kept in separate rooms and sometimes even in separate buildings.

All German casinos have the same entrance requirements. A player pays a standard five marks ($3) to enter, and except in hot weather the man must wear coat and tie. Casino taxes are high (up to 90 percent of gross gaming revenues), but at least the casinos do not have to worry about wages. Croupiers are paid entirely out of tip pools, and they are expected to stay at one casino for life! It almost sounds like a prison sentence. Other casinos will not even hire experienced dealers; they prefer to train them themselves. So if one gets fired, he might as well leave the country.

As a rule, the dealers are bilingual, and many of them speak English. One gaming analyst, who travels extensively, says this is the case in most European casinos. "That's a big problem I see. In the U.S., how many dealers can you find who can speak anything except English? Hell, some of them can barely speak *that!*"

Gambling in Europe is like going back to the mid-19th century. Even before entering a casino, the sights and sounds of another era surround you. There are outdoor concerts and narrow streets, little footbridges over gurgling rivers, and moss-covered buildings that are older than some American states. Couples walk slowly across sloping parks, and others play chess at outdoor cafes. There is a heady silence in the air, and people seem to smile for no reason at all.

The casino is just ahead, and our unidentified gaming consultant paints us a picture of what to expect as we start inside:

"First of all, an American would have a difficult time walking into one of these casinos. In the United States, he can put on a pair of Reeboks, cutoff shorts, and a raggedy T-shirt that says 'Harley Davidson' on it. In Europe, you'd better not look like Pee Wee Herman, or you won't even get in. It is something you would see in an old '40s movie when Cary Grant or George Raft would be wearing a tuxedo. Tuxedos are unusual in the states, but they are very common in Europe.

"As you walk in, you are greeted with opulence. You find a foyer that is done with tapestries and gorgeous paintings. Through parted velvet curtains you walk into the casino area, and not a word is heard. There is smiling, and conviviality, and not a drop of booze. If you want a drink, you go to a sequestered bar area. But it's tremendous alcohol. The wines are Lafayette Rothschild, whereas in Las Vegas if a guy gets himself some Boone's Farm he feels good. The cigars are Havanas, and readily available. Of course, it is all complimentary, as long as you have been wagering.

"The foods will boggle your mind. They serve Beluga caviar like we pass out chicken wings. An American might grab a handful and say it's terrible, not realizing that it costs more per ounce than platinum."

This is the big time...old world gambling with old world money. At Baden Baden, the list of signatures in the guest book reads like an almanac: the Windsors, King Saud, the Shah of Iran, King Hussein of Jordan, King Juan Carlos of Spain.

Unfortunately, there are just not enough kings and shahs to go around. Eruopean casino operators may scoff at Las Vegas, where gambling has only been legal for the blink of an eye. No one, however, can find fault with Nevada's formula for success. That formula includes volume business and a heavy dependence upon slot machines.

These Yankee monsters have already found their way to Monte Carlo, Austria, and the Netherlands, and they will soon be on the floors of French casinos. Five hundred

state-of-the-art slots have been ordered so far at Enghian-
les-Bains, just outside Paris, which until recently offered
only private baccara. If that is not enough to start World
War III, a casino in Germany is opening with slots, craps
and a European first — the "Big 6" money wheel!

In Austria, several casinos have started their own
"Megabucks" system, with a computerized setup offering a slot jackpot equivalent to $200,000. Croupiers there
were understandably upset, since their wages come from
tip pools. "And players don't tip machines," writer
William Thompson observed.

At Cannes, just the idea of putting slot machines in the
Palm Beach Casino was enough to cause dealers to stage
a walkout. They, too, work solely for tips. Interestingly
enough, dealers in Puerto Rico, who receive paid salaries
as well as tips, went on strike at about the same time. They
were not upset about slot machines, but something almost
as bad. Green peas were served three days in a row in their
staff dining room.

Gaming consultant Nigel Kent-Lemon, at a recent
speech in Las Vegas, classified casinos around the world
by category. Using his definitions, with a few comments
thrown in by other experts, we can get a fairly accurate
picture of gambling worldwide. Although, as Barry Quick
says, "A lot of the information (on international gaming)
is not available. One: you're not dealing with public corporations that are required to reveal their financial information. Two: you're not dealing with government
regulatory agencies that require casinos to make certain
information public."

Mickey Mouse Casinos: These are casinos that duck the
issue of legalized gambling. A perfect example is

Switzerland. As stipulated by a 1925 Swiss amendment, there can be only one "casino" in each Swiss state as long as the maximum payoff is five Swiss francs. In American currency, depending on fluctuation, that is anywhere from about 70 cents to $3.50. The only game in town is boule, a form of roulette, with six spins of the wheel every ten minutes. "Place your bets, ladies and gentlemen. Only four minutes to go."

Although Canada has lotteries and horse racing, other forms of gambling are frowned upon. There are several casinos in Canada, but the maximum bet allowed is $5, and the winnings are supposed to go to charity. There is also gambling on ferries that run from Vancouver to Seattle, where a 20-minute ride can take as long as three hours.

There are two casinos in Turkey, the Istanbul Hilton and the Turkiye Jockey Klubu. Both have table games, as well as slot machines with fixed jackpots. Tourists can gamble at anything; locals can only play the slots. In Morocco, the ground rules are a little different. Christians and Jews can gamble; Muslims cannot.

In Lebanon, gambling is considered to be against the Koran. However, there is a casino in Beirut. A gaming consultant tells how this came about. "Two brothers sold a parcel of land to a European. Consequently, the land was no longer considered to be hallowed ground, since it was now owned by a foreigner. Then the two brothers leased the land back and built a casino on it. And to this day, with all the fighting in Beirut, the place does not even have a bullet hole in it. It's nice to watch the sheiks drive up in their automobiles, and as they come through the door they remove their robes and headdresses. For a small period of time, they have stepped off the hallowed ground of the Koran onto the sacred ground of gambling."

Parasite Casinos: Falling into this category are European casinos designed expressly for tourists, including France, Monaco, Austria, Germany and Italy. With Switzerland surrounded on all sides by countries in the gambling business, the Swiss find themselves in the export business... the exportation of Swiss francs, that is. As one Swiss businessman said, "Our neighbors, with their casinos just across our borders, are quietly and politely picking our pockets." St. Vincent, Italy, which advertises itself as having the largest casino in Europe, has copied the tactics of Atlantic City — using tour buses to haul in additional trade.

Also classified as "parasite" casinos are the ones in the Caribbean, which draw their business from South America and the United States. Antigua and St. Maarten — where former Caesars Palace owner Clifford Perlman runs the Treasure Island Casino — bring in almost half their customers on chartered junkets.

As expected, casinos in Atlantic City fit into this category as well. Sixty million people live within gas-tank range of Atlantic City, and 1,200 buses a day bring in fresh meat from New York, Baltimore and Washington. Even more business is anticipated, once a high-speed rail connection to Philadelphia is completed and an international airport opens. Writer Sergio Lalli says the present facility, Bader Field, "was probably named after the guy who was holding the rope when the Hindenburg blew up."

Kent-Lemon said, "I can't believe anyone would go to Atlantic City if casinos open up elsewhere in the United States." His prediction is that by the year 2,000 ("Hopefully in my lifetime," he says) there will be legalized gambling across America. Other informed sources say gaming will eventually come to Florida, Louisiana, Michigan, and West Virginia. As this goes to press, there are only five states where some type of gambling is *not* allowed — Utah, Indiana, Idaho, Mississippi and Hawaii.

The biggest problem in Atlantic City, according to gaming expert Mike Sloan, is "oppressive regulatory controls." In New Jersey, there seems to be a regulation against everything. No poker games, no keno, no race and sports books, no topless showgirls, no drinks in cans or bottles, no cameras, no bathing suits, no slot machine seats.

Altogether, there are 1,200 enforcement people regulating the 12 Atlantic City casinos, while less than 400 oversee the 209 casinos in the whole state of Nevada. One legendary story concerns the time Caesars had to uproot all the tiles in its bathrooms. The New Jersey Casino Control Commission said the tiles were not "classy" enough.

Nevada casinos also fall into the "parasite" category. Thousands of San Francisco-area residents are bused into Reno and Lake Tahoe every week. Laughlin fills its casinos with people from Arizona and southern California. Las Vegas, meanwhile, still has enough charisma to draw record crowds from near and far. Over 16 million people visit Las Vegas each year, which is noteworthy because 1.6 million of them are conventioneers.

It seems ironic that while countries all over the world are promoting gambling to bolster tourism, Las Vegas is doing just the opposite. New ads go right for the jugular, but they do it discreetly. "Bring the family." "Fun in the sun." "The American way to play." Eventually, all the slot machines and craps tables may wind up in Europe, and the Europeans will have to come to Las Vegas just to get some peace and quiet.

Invisible Casinos: Casinos in Great Britain are termed as such, simply because they are "tolerated" by government. Restrictions, as noted earlier, include the ban of advertising and a 48-hour wait by new members before gambling. Gamblers must make their wagers with house chips, so consequently no one can step up to a gaming table and say, "Money plays," as they are allowed to do in the states. This, according to the Gaming Control Board, curbs impulse gambling, as does another regulation which prohibits casinos from extending additional credit to customers.

Casino games in England are a bit different than the ones in the United States, and this again is due to actions by the Gaming Control Board. Designed to give the gambler a more sensible bet for his money, the changes, though slight, are numerous.

For example, there is no "Big 6" or "Big 8" on the craps layouts; a player may take only single odds on all wagers; and hard-way bets pay an extra dollar. There is one zero on the roulette wheel, and if the zero comes up the player loses only half his bet on any even-money wagers. This drops the house percentage to a surprisingly low 1.35%, but as one gaming official said, "We make it up on volume."

Blackjack is even more complicated. Players cannot split 4's, 5's or 10's, and then can only split their cards one time. They cannot stand on any hand of 11 or less, which means they must have a "hard" total of 12 or a "soft" total of 17. Players can only insure blackjacks, and there is no "surrender" policy like the one in vogue at a few American casinos. British rules, incidentally, are universally followed so forget about shopping around for a better "deal."

There is no tipping allowed in English casinos, and it has been that way since the Gaming Control Board was formed in 1968. Before then, dealers received a small salary as well as a share of tips. The house took half the tips, and the rest was shared on a "point" system. A dealer might get one point, someone who dealt several games might get two points, a pit supervisor three points, and so on.

The result was sheer bedlam, according to a former dealer who was working in London at the time. "Everyone from the manager on down," he said, "was trying to stuff the toke box." The control board did not like the setup at all, and told the casinos in so many words to either give the dealers all their tip money or none. Not surprisingly, the casinos said, "None." Income dropped dramatically, and most of the good dealers left England for jobs in the Caribbean and United States. The average salary now is around $200 a week.

Unlike the United States, gambling winnings in England are non-taxable. This applies to all forms of legalized gambling except horse racing. In that sport, bettors can either pay a 5% tax after they win, or a 5% tax *before* they win. "It's really a scam," said one London resident. "Let's say a man bets $100 to win $1,000. If he pays his taxes before the race, it only costs him five percent of $100...or $5. If he waits until after the race, he pays five percent of $1,000...or $50." Of course, if he loses the bet, regardless of whether or not he has paid the taxes, it is still "Goodbye Mr. Chips."

England is not the only place in the world with "invisible" casinos. They also exist behind the Iron Curtain, in countries such as Bulgaria and Hungary. It seems that when it comes to hard Western currency, Karl Marx just doesn't have a chance. One gaming consultant, who was a tremendous help in putting this chapter together, said he once attended an amusement trade exposition in London. "My Swedish business partner introduced me to two men in ill-fitted suits. 'They would like you to take a look at the gambling equipment in their casino,' he told me.

"We flew to Finland on a commercial airliner. We were met there by a Lear jet, and we were in the air for another three hours. When we landed, it didn't take me long to realize we were inside Russia! It scared me at first, and I began waving my American passport about. This did not faze my newfound Soviet friends, who showed me a fistful of American dollars. 'This is the only thing we understand,' they told me. So regardless of what anyone says, yes Virginia, there *is* gambling in Russia."

Normal Casinos: These are casinos that are able to survive without importing customers from neighboring states or countries. The casinos are regulated, they are allowed to advertise, and they are out in the open where everyone can find them. Surprisingly, there are only three countries where casinos could be classified as "normal" operations. They include Holland, Australia and Spain.

There are 19 casinos in Spain, including the Casino Castillo de Perelada in Gerona, probably the most picturesque gambling joint in the world. Steeped in history, the casino is housed in a 14th century Spanish castle near the French border. It has a moat-like pond stocked with swans, an outdoor theater, a winery, a museum and a library filled with thousands of rare books and maps. It also has: 74 slot machines, one game of boule, seven French roulette wheels, two double zero American wheels, and four blackjack tables.

Gamblers in Holland can choose from 36 legal casinos,

and about 140 illegal ones. Hours are restricted in the privately-owned legal establishments, and patrons must adhere to the required dress code.

The country's top casinos include such linguistic mouthfuls as the Draf-En Renbaan Duindigt, the Nationale Stichting Casinospelen, and the Drafcentrum on Soestdijkerstraatweg Street in Hilversum. This brings to mind the time an American tourist sneezed while visiting the Hotel Nassauer Hof Gmbh in Frankfurt. "Gesundheit," said a passerby. "Oh," replied the tourist, "You speak English!"

According to gambling experts, Australia is one of the finest examples of proper casino management. The only problem in Australia, according to consultant Kent-Lemon, is obtaining a casino license. Here is the way it works in the outback:

"I would like a casino license."

"Who is your politician?"

"I don't have one."

"Forget it."

World Gaming At A Glance: In India, tourism officials say casinos are being planned at Kashmir, Bombay, Goa and Cochin. It is the age-old story, a way of scratching up more tourists and shoring up foreign trade. There is already gambling in Nepal, Korea, Belgium, Argentina, Greece, Africa, Turkey, Malaysia, Macao, Hong Kong, China and the Philipines. At the moment, however, there is so much political unrest in Manila that casino patrons are being body-searched.

Liechtenstein, Singapore, Switzerland, Andorra and Ireland are the only western jurisdictions without authentic casino facilities of some kind. Campaigns for full-fledged casinos persist in all of them except Liechtenstein, but the odds are bleak because of rigid constitutional provisions. Besides, how can something as mundane as gambling compete with such rousing fare as polka dances, yodel contests, and good ol' Irish whiskey?

CHAPTER 14

Looking Ahead

Over the years, Las Vegas has run into more flak than any other town in America. Gambling was sinful, shameful, spiteful. Then state lotteries caught on around the country like old smoldering forest fires, and suddenly gambling was wonderful, rightful, delightful.

Still, there is no place like Nevada. From time to time somebody will still let loose with another Nike missile, but it doesn't mean much anymore. Recently a Temple University College professor addressed a gaming conference in Reno and said: "Gambling is downright boring, and each year people become more and more bored with it." Sure, a few half-hearted vollies of return fire were loosened, but it was sort of like a water buffalo shaking its tail at a horsefly. So what if a college instructor thought gambling was boring. His idea of an exciting evening was probably turning his electric blanket on "high."

He never saw the Texas millionaire with a roll of bills the size of the Alamo. Every time the Texan lost a bet, he would laugh and peel off a few more hundreds. In twenty minutes he lost $23,000, and he was still laughing.

He never witnessed the well-dressed fellow who lost all his chips shooting craps, and then did a swan dive into the middle of the table. "He wasn't even drunk," a security guard said. "He was just teed-off because he lost."

He never heard the lady who stopped a dealer at the Frontier Hotel, where Sigfried and Roy were featured on the marquee. "Excuse me," she said. "Could you tell me what time Sigmund and Freud will be here?"

He never watched somebody keel over in a Vegas casino, because he forgot to sleep, or forgot to eat. Other gamblers are usually oblivious to it all, and on occasion have to be asked to step back so that emergency personnel can work over the fallen victim.

No, gambling may be many things, but it definitely is not boring. A person might find his values shuffled along with the cards, for just a day or two, or forget whether it is night or day. . .and not even really care. Eventually he may tire of it all, like a kid with too much Christmas candy, but he will never find his mind wandering. If so, then there are over 15 million bored tourists ho-humming into Las Vegas every year, with that number expected to double by the end of the century.

In fact, the biggest boom since the siege of the '60s has already hit Las Vegas. Practically every hotel on the Strip is sticking on floors and adding on wings, getting ready for the onslaught:

The Landmark is building a 720-room tower.

The El Rancho is constructing a 13-story highrise with 587 new rooms.

The Dunes is adding 1,200 rooms.

The Sahara is putting up a 575-room tower.

The Flamingo is building a 722-room addition.

The Holiday Casino is building 2,300 additional rooms and a new hotel tower, which will make it the largest

Holiday Inn in the world.

Bally's is spending $200 million reshaping its Las Vegas resort, making it the first billion-dollar hotel in the world.

The Riviera has added a 35-story 1,702-room addition, making it the tallest building in the state and the largest hotel in the world.

The new Mirage is now up on the Strip next to Caesars Palace. Built at a cost of nearly $500 million, it has 3,272 rooms and a 60,000-square foot casino.

Circus Circus has built a $300 million casino at the south end of the Strip. Named "Excalibur," this 47-acre resort is laid out like a European castle.

Not to be outdone, Caesars is spending $175 million to build a shopping compound bigger than the original Coliseum in Rome. Et tu, you guys.

Other casino projects on the drawing board include the Carnival Hotel, a 3,000-room resort near the Aladdin; and Southstar, an ambitious network of ten hotels south of the Hacienda. The whole setup is becoming a twisted tangle of comings and goings. Eventually city cab drivers will have to take refresher courses, just to keep track of what's where!

Another twist in the tangle deals with ownership of what's already here. A case in point is Summa Corporation, the old Howard Hughes conglomerate that at one time owned almost as much of Nevada as the U.S. government, including a half dozen resorts on the Vegas Strip. Summa had a super liquidation sale in 1987, selling the Castaways to Steve Wynn, who owns the Golden Nugget; the Frontier and the Silver Slipper to Margaret Elardi, who used to own the Pioneer Club in Las Vegas and now owns the Pioneer Hotel in Laughlin; the Sands and the Desert

Inn to Kirk Kerkorian, who built the International, which became the Las Vegas Hilton, and built the MGM Grand Hotel, which is now Bally's (Kerkorian, incidentally, resold the Sands to someone else but kept the Desert Inn and put the MGM logo on the Desert Inn's chips). During the same year, Japanese millionaire Katsuki Manabe bought the Holiday International in downtown Las Vegas, which he renamed the Park Hotel and Casino; Japanese millionaire Masao Nangaku bought the Dunes from John Anderson, who also owns the Maxim; Japanese millionaire Ginji Yasuda took over the Aladdin, which he purchased from Ed Torres, the owner of the El Rancho.

All together now — ARRRGHHIIIIII!

The invasion by the Japanese came about because of an American trade deficit, which resulted in a firmer currency rate overseas. Suddenly the Japanese had more yen than they knew what to do with. Nangaku, for example, had already parlayed an electric appliance company into a whirlwind empire that included a string of bowling alleys in Japan, a Tokyo art museum, and eleven hotels around the world. Not only did he pay $155 million for the Dunes Hotel, but another $200 million was earmarked for improvements to the rundown property. Plans call for an indoor park; three gleaming towers veneered in red, green and blue marble; and 1,200 new rooms.

The Dunes was once known as "the jewel of the Strip," but over the years the hotel had fallen on hard times. It was difficult to explain, because the Dunes was situated on the choicest corner in Las Vegas. Forty thousand pedestrians a day hotfoot it from Caesars Palace to the Barbary Coast to Bally's to the Flamingo to the Dunes. The rest of the hotels were doing a landslide business, yet the mighty Dunes Hotel was in the hands of the U.S. Bankruptcy Court.

So on a sweltering Tuesday in 1988, the ax fell.

By registered mail, the notices went to 2,055 men and women. "At 11:59 p.m. on June 30, M&R Investment Company will no longer operate the Dunes Hotel. As a result, M&R will terminate all of its employees... and cease providing major medical, life, dental, vision, and disability plan coverages as well."

It was the final death rattle of a company that had botched and blundered its way through two decades of casino ownership, and suddenly over 2,000 people were out of work. The employees did not walk away empty-handed, however. Each received a personal memo from Dunes President Burton Cohen.

"As the time draws nearer to midnight, June 30, when M&R Investment Co. will no longer operate and manage the Dunes Hotel, the Management and Board of Directors want to say 'thank you' for your loyal and conscientious service over the past few years." The memo ended with this lamentable postscript: "Don't forget to pick up your final paycheck at the Time Office."

Morale was so low at the Dunes during this period that workers initiated a "termination stakes" betting sheet on who would stay once Nangaku's management team took over. Odds ranged from 65-1 for a shift boss to even money on pit clerks and chip runners. It was black humor at best, but as one blackjack floorman said, "The one thing you learn in this business is just to worry about yourself."

The Dunes employees were processed by Clark Management Company, which was headed by Dennis Gomes. Gomes had a squeaky clean reputation. He headed the Audit Division of the Nevada Gaming Control Board, then was named to supervise the Special Investigations Bureau for the New Jersey Gaming Enforcement Division. Later

he was Executive Vice-President of Casino Operations at
the Frontier Hotel; Senior Vice-President in charge of
Casino Operations at the Hilton Corporation; Executive
Vice-President and Chief Operating Officer of the Aladdin Hotel. Dunes employees were elated. At last, after years
of loyalty and sacrifice, they would finally become an in-
tegral part of a successful casino operation.

Clark Management's staff interviewed all non-union personnel, and a week later almost 95 percent of the employees
were rehired. To the 167 workers who were terminated, it
was a shaky step into the unknown. To the new owners,
it was cold blue-steeled logic. Multiply 167 jobs by an
average yearly salary of $20,000, and the savings is over $3
million. "This is a sacrifice we have to make," said one of
the new executives. "Unfortunately, it's a sign of the
times."

Then again, it was not Clark Management's fault that
the Dunes was leaking like an old ship. The hotel, built at
a cost of $4 million, opened in 1955, and ran into finan-
cial difficulties almost immediately. It closed in January
of 1956, then opened again in May of that year as the M&R
Investment Company.

1969 — Continental Connector Corporation takes over
the Dunes in a $59 million stock transfer. The Securities
and Exchange Commission charges the new owners with
defrauding stockholders.

1975 — St. Louis attorney Morris Shenker buys an interest in the Dunes.

1976 — Shenker sues the Teamsters Union for $140
million, claiming the union backed out of a $40 million loan
commitment. The suit is thrown out of court.

1979 — Shenker denies allegations by the FBI that Kansas City crime syndicate has a concealed interest in the Dunes.

1982 — Shenker sells the Dunes to Stuart and Clifford Perlman for $185 million. The sale collapses the following year.

1983 — A federal jury orders Shenker to repay a $34 million loan to the Culinary Union.

February 1984 — The IRS bills Shenker $66 million for unpaid taxes stretching back 20 years. Shenker files for personal bankruptcy.

March 1984 — Valley Bank of Nevada lends the Dunes $68 million.

May 1984 — California farmer John Anderson buys a controlling interest in the Dunes, leaving Shenker with 26 percent.

February 1985 — The Dunes is cited for failing to meet fire safety standards, and spends $2.2 million on retrofitting.

September 1985 — The Dunes defaults on the $68 million bank loan, and Valley Bank moves ahead with legal steps required for foreclosure.

November 1985 — The Dunes files for reorganization under Chapter 11.

The Dunes was not the only Las Vegas resort to find itself protected by the courts from panting creditors. Although the screenplays were rewritten, and the cast of characters altered, there were other big casinos with problems of their own: the Stardust, Fremont, Sands, Aladdin, Marina, Landmark, and Riviera.

The Riviera stayed in bankruptcy for two years, a glum turn of events for the city's first high-rise. Meshulam Riklis, who bought the resort on a whim in 1973, had amassed a crippling debt load that nothing seemed to overcome. In order to get more people into the place, he stocked the showroom with big-name movie stars. Dolly Parton was paid an outlandish $350,000 a week. All this did was put the hotel further in hock.

The turning point at the Riviera came in 1985, when Arthur Waltzman was appointed to head operations. The debt structure was reorganized, operating costs were minimized, and the red carpet was rolled out for grind customers that other Strip hotels had long ignored. Dolly Parton was replaced with Pia Zadora, who would probably have worked for free — since Pia Zadora is the current senora of — Meshulam Riklis!

Now the Riviera is literally on top of the world, spending $100 million expanding its resort and adding a curved, oblong tower that will be the tallest in Nevada. For the Riviera, the nightmare was over.

When Kirk Kerkorian bought the Sands and the Desert Inn in late 1987, a rosy picture was painted in local newspapers. However, down near the end of the story was this small paragraph:

Employees were told that Kerkorian's people will be arriving as early as Thursday to inspect the properties and meet with employees. It was said most of the employees will be offered the chance to remain in their positions under the new owners.

Most of the employees will get to keep their jobs, the story says. What the story does not say is that *some* of the employees are going to get the old heave-ho without so much as a perfunctory two-weeks notice. Granted, most of them will be from the old management team, but that is small consolation to everyone else in the organization. Once again, the guy at the bottom of the totem pole is shaking in his boots, filling out job applications all over town. . . just in case. All he knows is that some rich tycoon bought the hotel, and his $150 a week (plus tips) might be headed for somebody else's pocket.

Morale, or the lack of it, has always been a problem in Las Vegas. . . and every time a casino files for bankruptcy, or is sold, the old merry-go-round starts all over again. One casino owner ran through 45,000 employees in twelve years, so how is a cocktail waitress at another resort going to feel when she reads in the paper that he bought the place?

How does a security guard feel when he gets a paycheck and cannot get it cashed at his own bank?

How does a slot floorman feel when he looks at the new schedule and he is only working three days?

How does a dealer feel when he finds out his casino is returning to single-deck blackjack, and he has to go back to school?

How does a pit clerk feel when new owners make her sign an employment appication that says: "I hereby understand and agree that employment beyond any probationary period shall not result in heightened expectation of continued employment."

How does a dealer at the Nevada Club in Reno feel when Lincoln Management buys the casino and fires everyone, and he gets hired back later at a cut in pay with the loss of earned benefits?

How does a pit boss at Harold's Club in Reno feel when

he and 700 others are terminated by new owners, and then reads where the new owner says, "We purchased Harold's Club's assets, and not the employees."

The hotels do not suffer. They are nothing more than big impersonal buildings with exotic names and fancy marquees. The people who *work* there are the ones who suffer. Pushed against the wall by the IRS, deserted in the trenches by their own employers, the workers feel abandoned. Stripped of benefits by new owners, unable to collect unemployment benefits because of legal technicalities, uninsured and unrewarded, the workers feel deserted.

Perhaps that is why new Dunes owner Masao Nangaku, in a statement that followed his purchase of the Las Vegas resort, said an important element of his work would be a personnel policy "that puts the employee first." As his attorney later explained, "To Mr. Nangaku, the employee is part of his family. He plans on honoring the present union contracts and he wants the employees to be happy with the Dunes."

Dennis Gomes elaborated on Nangaku's philosophy by saying, "A good management team is concerned about the people who work for them. It can't be faked, it's got to be real. The top person has to be a genuinely caring person. If he is, then everything he does will reflect that, and the people he has surrounding him will reflect that. And the employees are going to be happy."

One of the first moves by Gomes was to institute a new management system, giving workers the chance to communicate problems and complaints directly to him. Terminated workers can now go before a committee of fellow employees, and not even Gomes can overrule the committee's final decision. It is a far cry from what is happening elsewhere in the industry.

Gomes was considered a revolutionary when he first moved into casino management, but now many of his ideas have become standard procedure. "Casino people concentrated for many years on their uniqueness. They lost track of all the sophisticated business tools that other industries had been using for years. Now that things have become more competitive, people began applying those techniques in the casino."

As an example, Gomes cited the interplay between computers and the casino rating system. "When I first talked about using the computer in calculating the theoretical win, everybody thought I was crazy. Now they are all using computers to rate players — to discriminate between good and bad players, those who deserve complimentaries and those who don't. That's where your profit margin is."

When Gomes went to the Las Vegas Hilton in 1984, the sprawling property was in a "gigantic profit slump. It was very simple for us to turn it around because it had such tremendous facilities. It just needed a different marketing orientation and better management. When we provided that, the (result) was automatic." With Gomes at the helm, profits soared from $17 million to $48 million in three short years. "The facility was the same and the location was the same, so it just shows how important management can be." Location is critical, Gomes admits, counting off properties on his fingers as though they were three for a dollar. "Caesars Palace, Bally's, the Dunes. . . they're all in the best location in town. But without good management, you can see that some of them don't do too well."

Caesars Palace is far and away the city's most popular resort, even though it never has followed the effective guidelines of other casino operations. "Caesars for years had very few rooms," Gomes said, "and it was still successful. That's where you generate the revenue. You can see by example what happened at the Flamingo and the downtown Golden Nugget, and almost every place in town. Where they've added rooms, they've added revenue. You generate so much gaming revenue per person, in addition to room revenue and food and beverage revenue.'' As to how a small Vegas casino can compete with one the size of Dallas or Fort Worth, Gomes believes it is possible. ''But it has to find its own niche. It would have to be some type of specialty operation, like a hotel that caters to a certain market segment.''

New marketing ideas have also helped Las Vegas struggle through one of the most trying times of the year: that peculiar gaming industry affliction known as ''December.'' It was always a white Christmas in Las Vegas. A dealer would open his ''toke'' envelope, and his face would turn white. December was the lull before New Year's, when every car on the Strip had Nevada license plates... and both of them were headed out of town. A tourist once called a hotel showroom captain the week before Christmas. ''What time is your show tonight?'' the tourist asked. The showroom captain answered, ''What time can you be here?''

Now December means the National Finals Rodeo at the Thomas & Mack coliseum, the Grand Prix of Poker at the Golden Nugget, The Great Slot Round-Up at Caesars Palace. The Tropicana has a $75,000 craps tournament, with the winner getting the hotel's version of a Super Bowl ring. ''How'd you get that ring, grandpa?'' ''I threw a pass... with $2,000 on the line.''

It all started in 1978, when the Sahara Hotel launched a casino tournament to beef up Christmas trade. The tourney was a clamoring triumph, and now tourists are able to pick and choose from a dozen other year-end events.

Something is missing, though, from this majestic manifest of marketing techniques, management philosophies, and all the rest. Call it charisma, or showmanship . . . or maybe "pizzazz" is the right word. Jay Sarno had it. Ted Turner had it and sold it to Donald Trump. Howard Hughes had it, and didn't want it. Dan Rather wanted it, and didn't have it. Gary Hart thought he had it. Ted Kennedy had it, and lost it. Marilyn Monroe oozed it. Joe Namath fumbled it. Florence Nightingale nursed it. Greta Garbo cursed it. Now, like a priceless flagon of youth elixir, it is within the grasp of a bold trailblazer named Steve Wynn.

Wynn graduated from college in 1963, and moved to Las Vegas four years later as a stockholder in the Frontier Hotel. According to one news release, "While studying hotel administration at UNLV, he worked as a fry-cook, hotel clerk, bell captain and night auditor." (In other words, if he stayed out of hot water there was room at the top, as long as he carried his own weight, and went by the book.) After the Frontier was sold, Wynn set up a statewide liquor distributorship . . . which he liquidated for a hefty profit in 1971. That was when he became hotel manager at the Horseshoe Club, working under the wing of the legendary Benny Binion. Three years later, he and six other investors bought the Golden Nugget across the street. The new corporation's president was Steve Wynn.

Wynn revolutionized the industry, concentrating not on the pompous Las Vegas Strip but on the overlooked and oftentimes neglected downtown area. He gave new cars to company officers and shares of stock to employees, and spent a shocking $60 million transforming his hotel into a kind of 20th-century Taj Mahal. His comment at the time was, ''You've got to have romance, and the Golden Nugget is the sexiest place there is.'' In 1980, he spent $75 million building the Golden Nugget Hotel & Casino in Atlantic City. Seven years later, he dumped his New Jersey holdings for a profit of $365 million. He spent $120 million expanding the Golden Nugget in downtown Las Vegas, then bulldozed the Castaways to start construction of The Mirage, his new half-billion dollar resort on the Strip. Steve Wynn was 46 years old.

''In order to do projects of this nature you have to feel secure,'' he said recently. ''I don't have that visceral feeling of security in New Jersey that I do in Las Vegas.'' Wynn believes Atlantic City will never rival Nevada, and shrugs at the New Jersey city's claim of 30 million visitors a year.

''Let's face it,'' he says. ''Atlantic City is the local crap game for New York, Philadelphia and New Jersey. It's a day trip. At our Golden Nugget back there, we ran a survey and found that 60 percent of our guests came down every week or ten days. So, when they talk about 30 million visitors, it's pretty clear to me that they're talking about maybe a million people coming in 30 times a year.''

Just ten years ago, no one would have believed Wynn. Atlantic City was a genuine threat to Las Vegas, a national recession was slapping the city with muffled repercussions, gasoline prices were up, tourism was down, and there were ugly rumors that some states would introduce lotteries. Wynn was one of the first to panic, and still owns 14 acres in Atlantic City in case he ever decides to go back.

He laughs about it now, though. ''It turned out that Las Vegas was more galvanized and powerful than anyone thought. The image of the town as a resort destination was so strong that we weren't really in any trouble at all.'' Consequently, Wynn has no qualms about spending money like water...signing Siegfried and Roy to a five-year contract for $57 million, and paying out $6.9 million just on elevators for his new resort.

When he talks about his new hotel, his eyes light up, and his boyish enthusiasm leaves little doubt that this new casino will be something special:

"I'm driving down the Strip in my car. It's at night. The Caesars Palace fountains are spewing into the sky, lit by turquoise lights — St. Peter's Square, recreated by Jay Sarno. Dead ahead is something...I make a left-hand turn, and I drive up the driveway. And there's this 40-foot waterfall dropping clear in front of me beyond the porte cochere. There's 30 feet of palm trees on top of that. There's an eight-story mountain rising up in front of me with a waterfall that looks like Angel Falls.''

You can almost hear the water splash off moss-covered rocks as Wynn goes on. "It will have a British colonial look to it. Bermuda. High louvered shutters. Palm trees. The tropics. Tradewinds. South Sea islands. Hawaii. Lagoons...''

Wynn's new resort, along with Southstar and the Carnival, will give the city an additional 12,000 hotel rooms. Another 7,000 rooms will be added by existing hotels after their expansions are completed. Ironically, all of this comes at a time when the national trend is toward smaller hotel projects with fewer rooms. The end is probably still not in sight. At last report, weekend occupancy in Las Vegas hotels was averaging 92 percent year-round. "Where else would I get a chance to do a project like this?'' Wynn asks. "You can't spend $440 million on a regular hotel. Only in Nevada, only in the gaming world can you do something like this. It can be the most profitable place on earth.''

Statistics compiled by the Las Vegas Convention Authority lend credence to Wynn's words. Not only do 16 million people stream into Las Vegas each year, but an unbelievable $8.6 billion is pumped into the local economy. Taking these facts into consideration, Steve Wynn's new Mirage does not seem like much of a gamble at all.

What turned Las Vegas around more than anything was a high-powered new advertising campaign that touted southern Nevada as a kind of bargain basement paradise. Less emphasis was placed on gambling, and more on extolling Las Vegas as a family-oriented vacation spot. Marketing strategists used superstar entertainers to flood airwaves and magazine pages with such hoop-de-doo as: "Las Vegas, the American Way to Play." (A good American would not be caught *dead* in Atlantic City, much less in some foreign country where terrorists lurked on every street corner.)

It was all worked out very carefully, and nobody was safe. The eight million dollar ad campaign featured Frank Sinatra and Bill Cosby for the jet-setters, Kool and the Gang for the black audience, the McGuire Sisters for the over-55 crowd, and a country and western group for anyone else that got left out. The campaign also focused on overseas audiences, with ads in European publications and Japanese TV commercials.

The whole thing comes under the auspices of the Las Vegas Convention and Visitors Authority, which has devised other underhanded undertakings to keep the city from being underestimated. A positive image of Las Vegas is underlined, conventions and trade shows in other cities are under scrutiny, a five-year marketing plan is under development, and the environment is underplayed so that tourism is not undermined. Even the Downtown Progress Association is understanding, although that might be an understatement. "We've embarked on our own individual marketing campaign," says Marketing Director Gary Morris. "I don't see anything ahead but uninterrupted growth and prosperity. Everything is hot downtown." Then, somewhat ominously, he added, "Knock on wood."

Las Vegas is taking slow, sure steps this time. There is always that chilling possibility of a room surplus like the one that brought Las Vegas to its knees in the '60s. Then again, as Dennis Gomes said: "We've gone through that for 50 years. People say we're overbuilding, but the pace of customers always overcomes that. The town becomes saturated with customers, then there's another building boom, and another glut of rooms. But I don't think we'll ever be in a position where we have permanently over-built." With a chuckle he added, "Besides, that estimate of Las Vegas having another 20,000 rooms in the next couple of years was a decent estimate based on what everybody was saying. If you look at inside information, it looks like only half of those rooms will really be there."

Still, with all the hoopla and fanfare about the "new" Las Vegas — the "family" Las Vegas — there is a longing deep inside for the old bygone times when the town had real class, personality. . .and a certain kind of intimacy. But will all the new hotel rooms be full, or will a host of new bankruptcies permeate the local news. *Taking care of the customer*, that's what it's all about. If the casinos gouge too many customers, there *will* be empty rooms and there *will* be chaos. The lesson will have been repeated for all of those who weren't paying attention the first time. Steve Wynn will say in his bubbly way that things are better now, that "almost all of the folks who come to Las Vegas are really coming for the Grand Canyon, or the weather, or the entertainment and the shows, or they're en route to somewhere else." That does not necessarily sit well with the old-timers who remember when a $100 chip was a tip and not somebody's whole bankroll, and tourists gaped when they thought they saw a gangster. Mario Puzo described that exciting era in a single sentence: "Money and beautiful women zinged together like magnets," he said. The atmosphere was electric, and the casinos bulged with movie stars and high rollers. A few still graze contentedly in gourmet restaurants, but today they are called "preferred customers" and — Heaven help us — "large gamers."

The big craze now is chasing after the slot crowd, and jackpots are rewarded with bonuses like nylon hose, boxes of candy, and free Whopperburgers. Circus Circus slops up 17,000 buffet meals a day, and reserves blackjack tables for non-smokers. It works out fine, because most of the players are too young to smoke anyway. The Frontier has 40,000 members in its Slot Club, and if a person has enough "pull" he can see a free show or get a casino rate on a room. Most of the casinos have even taken the old "lemon" symbol off the machines to get rid of the town's sour, and thus negative, image. Bookkeepers have been replaced by statistics junkies, casino owners live in Tokyo or Beverly Hills, and gambling is just something else to do in Las Vegas, "Gateway to the great Southwest." It is a far cry indeed from the time when Las Vegas was "the entertainment capital of the world." Now the city is only a stop on the way to Disneyland or Sea World, just a place to spend the weekend.

Oh, there is a good side to it all. Bigger profits, sure. More tourists. A population of over a million by the year 2000. A city of retirees on the outskirts of town, red-tiled roofs rising from the foothills. People Movers shuttling tourists across downtown, and to the Strip, and to the airport. A superspeed bullet train hurtling from southern California to Vegas at speeds of up to 300 miles an hour. Neat little slot machines that will take credit cards instead of cash.

It is just so...precise, and maybe that is the problem. One cannot help but feel a certain yearning for the time when things were simpler, though perhaps more volatile. Certainly the town was a lot more colorful when a future president of the United States headlined an all-star revue at the Last Frontier. Ronald Reagan got $5,500 for one week's work, $1,650 more than he would get 25 years later in the White House.

The town was a lot more glamorous when there were stars in the showrooms that people had actually *heard* of. Peggy Lee, Johnny Carson, Barbra Streisand. Now billboards are cluttered with parentheses. Suzanne Somers (Three's Company), Bowser (Sha Na Na), Frankie Valli (The Four Seasons)...and "The King" is no longer Sinatra, but some kid named Newton.

The town was a lot more exciting when casinos were bankrolled right out of the pockets of individual owners, or working partners, who knew all the dealers by their first names. Now practically every resort in Las Vegas is a corporation merger, and the future of the city hinges on Wall Street and even border skirmishes halfway around the world.

The town was a lot more impressive when a 30-foot

Sultan stood over the bold Dunes Hotel, arms folded and defiant. Times change...and maybe the Sultan saw it coming. In the '60s, he towered over the hotel's front entrance. In the '70s, he was relegated to the back lot — standing guard over a golf course, of all things. By the '80s, he was old and decrepit, patches of gray plaster showing beneath his turban. Then one day a rainstorm came, and the old Sultan went tumbling down...finished mercifully by a lightning bolt, square between the eyes.

We miss you, big fella.

Bibliography

All About Blackjack, John Gollehon. G.P. Putnam's Sons, New York, N.Y., 1985.

All About Baccarat, John Gollehon. G.P.Putnam's Sons, New York, N.Y., 1985.

House Of Cards, Jerome Skolnick. Little, Brown and Company, Boston, Mass., 1978.

Gambling Scams, Darwin Ortiz. Dodd, Mead & Company, New York, New York, 1984.

Casino Management, Bill Friedman. Lyle Stuart Inc., Secaucus, New Jersey, 1982.

Dummy Up And Deal, Lee Solkey. GBC Press, Las Vegas, Nevada, 1980.

Las Vegas: The Entertainment Capital, Donn Knepp. Lane Publishing Company, Menlo Park, California, 1987.

Marketing Bulletin, Las Vegas Convention and Visitors Authority, 1986.

Las Vegas Visitor Profile Study, Las Vegas Convention and Visitors Authority, 1987.

Marketing Report, Reno-Sparks Convention and Visitors Authority, 1986.

Loose Change Blue Book, Daniel R. Mead. Mead Publishing Corporation, Long Beach, California, 1986/1987.

Gaming Nevada Style, Nevada Gaming Commission & State Gaming Control Board, Carson City, Nevada, 1982.

Scarne's New Complete Guide To Gambling, John Scarne. Simon and Schuster, New York, New York, 1974.

Reno-Sparks, Nevada, A Mini-History, Phyllis and Lou Zauner. Zanel Publications, Tahoe Paradise, Calif., 1978.

Mark Twain In Virginia City, Samuel Clemens. Nevada Publications, Las Vegas, Nevada, 1985.

Las Vegas SUN Newspaper, selected articles, 1987/1988.

Las Vegas REVIEW/JOURNAL Newspaper, selected articles, 1987/1988.

SPORTS FORM, selected articles, Dirson Enterprises, Las Vegas, Nevada, 1988.

Los Angeles TIMES, selected articles, 1987.

Gollehon books you'll enjoy reading...

Las Vegas Behind The Tables, by Barney Vinson, $5.95. The original bestseller that created controversy in its "tell all" style.

Written by a 20-year casino veteran, this one-of-a-kind book takes the reader beyond the facade of slot machines and flashing neon, sizing up all the games from the casino's viewpoint, and providing a rare perspective that few players ever see.

An entire chapter is devoted to an interview with disgruntled dealers, letting them tell in no uncertain terms what it's really like to work "behind the tables."

His book is peppered with humorous anecdotes about superstitious casino bosses and famous players.

Atlantic City Behind The Tables, by John Alcamo, $5.95. The third new book in Gollehon's "Behind The Tables" series.

Fifteen intriguing chapters cover just about everything, including "The World's Highest Roller," a man who typically bets $100,000 per hand! The author's play-by-play report on this billionaire's action is pure delight.

A thought-provoking chapter deals with memory experts, and the potential for these people to use their talent against the casino.

Video Poker Mania, by Dwight & Louise Crevelt, $4.95. A hot new sequel to the authors' bestselling *Slot Machine Mania,* based on the authors' beliefs that most players are being duped into playing the wrong strategies to win.

Co-author Dwight Crevelt is a veteran designer and engineer of today's high-tech slot machines, and the only author to have written on this subject from inside the slot industry.

As proof of their contention, the authors cite internal information that confirms a glaring fact that few players know: *Video poker machines are holding a much larger percentage of profit for the casinos than they're supposed to!*

Their discovery has led them to devise a set of *three* new strategies, based on different types of players and different methods of play. They no longer believe that one strategy is right for everyone. Find out which new strategy is right for you!

Slot Machine Mania, by Dwight & Louise Crevelt, $4.95. Slot machines are the fastest growing segment of the casino and sure to get bigger. It's been estimated that over 30 million people in the U.S. are frequent players. *Slot Machine Mania* is perfect for these players as the most comprehensive, up-to-date volume on slots and video poker!

Virtually everything is covered: how to judge percentages and select more favorable machines; money management; common misconceptions; superstitions; cheating methods and regulations; casino promotions; and million-dollar jackpot winners.

Beat The Track, by Ada Kulleck, $4.95. *Beat The Track* stands out among the hodge-podge of horse-racing books now on the market. Covering both thoroughbred-racing and harness-racing, the author writes from the heart to give the reader a sincere and realistic understanding of what it's like to bet and handicap horses.

Carefully structured for both the novice and serious player, the author details her two-decade success at Southern California tracks, from how to read the Daily Racing Form, to how to eliminate losers. Her logical, sensible, easy-to-learn methods have fooled the most respected handicappers.

Lifestyles Of A High Roller, by Phyllis Wolff, $5.95. Experience what it's like to be treated like royalty; to have the casino cater to your every need. From lavish suites to limo service; from ringside seats at all the shows to gourmet dining every evening... you'll meet celebrities, attend VIP parties, and enjoy high-stakes action in the casino.

As the wife of one of the casino's most sought-after high rollers, the author presents a diary account of their many exciting trips to Las Vegas, Atlantic City, the Bahamas... wherever the action is non-stop, and the treatment is fit for a king.

Off The Strip, by Moe Shuckelman and Mark Lewis, $4.95. A collection of gambling jokes and cartoons that makes for a truly unique book. You'll laugh at these great cartoons by Mark Lewis who covers just about everything from video poker to swim-up blackjack tables. And Moe Shuckelman's jokes poke fun at just about everyone, from pit bosses to sore losers. *Off The Strip* is a refreshing break from the serious side of the games. Makes a great gift!

Las Vegas & Reno Area Fun Guide, by Derotha Sourwine, $3.95. Written by a born-and-raised Nevada writer, the FUN GUIDE's "inside" advantage really comes through in the many personal tips to the reader that only a "local" could offer. Her "very readable" style is a refreshing change of pace from the typical travel guide or simple directory.

In addition, the reader will truly enjoy the author's expression of Nevada's natural scenic beauty from the intriguing desert to the High Sierras... from Lake Mead to Lake Tahoe... from nearby Death Valley to the Grand Canyon.

Special attention is given to attractions the entire family — especially the kids — will enjoy, from theme parks to the famous Ponderosa Ranch.

Casino Games, by John Gollehon, $5.95. The only mass-market paperback that covers *all* the games: blackjack, craps, roulette, baccarat, keno, video poker, slot machines, and sports betting!

Casino Games differs vastly from all the other "how to play" books because simply knowing "how to play" isn't enough. What makes this book a strong seller is the author's critical commentary on discipline, money management, and common sense; how to recognize an opportunity that most players never see.

Gollehon teaches the reader *how to win!*

The Book Of Famous Places, by Diane Burton Robb, $5.95. Perhaps the most unique travel book on the market, *The Book Of Famous Places* is a travel guide, history book, and reference book to our nation's historic sites.

Divided into three sections: Wars, Discovery, and Presidents, this fascinating book covers our history in a most readable way, providing rare insight into historically famous personalities and little known facets of history-making events. Sure to be a hit with trivia fans too!

Gollehon books are available at many of the leading national-chain bookstores and at hotel and airport newsstands. The publisher regrets it cannot fulfill orders directly from the consumer except for quantity orders (contact: Special Sales). If a book is unavailable at your favorite bookstore, tell them to order it through Baker & Taylor or Ingrams for prompt delivery usually within 48 hours.

Prices, availability, and book specifications subject to change without notice.